DEATH OF A PARENT

In the midst of the busiest years of our lives and careers, just as many of us are beginning to confront our own aging, we are likely to lose a parent – and as commonplace, even expected, as such an event may be, the repercussions can be dramatic. This book is the first to set out in clear and comprehensive terms what the death of a parent means to most adults – how it in fact functions as a turning point in our emotional, social, and personal lives. Drawing on her own groundbreaking research, in-depth interviews, and data collected nationwide, Dr. Debra Umberson explores the social and psychological factors that determine how this important loss will affect us – as a personal crisis or an opportunity for healthy change. Her book shows how adults, far from the "finished" beings we are often assumed to be, can be profoundly transformed by the death of a parent – in beliefs, behavior, goals, sense of self – transformed in ways that will continue to affect us, for better or worse, for the rest of our lives.

Debra Umberson is Professor and Chair of Sociology at the University of Texas at Austin. Her research for *Death of a Parent* was supported by a FIRST Award from the National Institute on Aging. As a former social worker, Dr. Umberson has worked with terminally ill patients and their families. She is the author of thirty-six articles and chapters on family relationships and health, and she lectures on issues of death and dying at the University of Texas.

This book is dedicated to all of my parents:
Bill and Wilma Umberson,
David and Judy Steiker,
and
Grannie

DEATH OF A PARENT

Transition to a New Adult Identity

DEBRA UMBERSON

University of Texas

CAMBRIDGE
UNIVERSITY PRESS

PUBLISHED BY THE PRESS SYNDICATE OF THE UNIVERSITY OF CAMBRIDGE
The Pitt Building, Trumpington Street, Cambridge, United Kingdom

CAMBRIDGE UNIVERSITY PRESS
The Edinburgh Building, Cambridge CB2 2RU, UK
40 West 20th Street, New York, NY 10011-4211, USA
477 Williamstown Road, Port Melbourne, VIC 3207, Australia
Ruiz de Alarcón 13, 28014 Madrid, Spain
Dock House, The Waterfront, Cape Town 8001, South Africa

http:// www.cambridge.org

First published 2003

Printed in the United States of America

Typefaces Goudy 11.5/16 pt., FC Village, and OPTISerlio   *System* LATEX 2$_\varepsilon$ [TB]

A catalog record for this book is available from the British Library.

Library of Congress Cataloging in Publication Data
Umberson, Debra.
Death of a parent : transition to a new adult identity / Debra Umberson.
p.   cm.
Includes bibliographical references and index.
ISBN 0-521-81338-7
1. Parents – Death – Psychological aspects.   2. Loss (Psychology)
3. Adulthood – Psychological aspects.   I. Title.
BF789.D4 U48   2003
155.9′37′0854–dc21   2002035084

ISBN 0 521 81338 7 hardback

CONTENTS

ACKNOWLEDGMENTS

Many bereaved adults shared their thoughts and feelings to help me understand the experience of losing a parent. I am most grateful to all of the men and women who donated their time and opened up their lives to provide the material I needed to write this book.

Colleagues from around the country facilitated this project in various ways. My Texas colleague, Christine Williams, provided advice about qualitative methods and the handling of in-depth interviews. She also provided helpful comments on the first and last drafts of this book. Thanks to her for lighting matches to set sociology on fire. Thanks to Kristi Williams, of the Ohio State University, for her energy, enthusiasm, distraction, and great ideas on numerous projects over the past several years. I am particularly indebted to James S. House of the University of Michigan for his mentorship, for including me on the Americans' Changing Lives (ACL) project, and for providing access to the ACL data. The ACL data collection was supported by the National Institute on Aging (James S. House, Principal Investigator, NIA AGO5562).

Meichu D. Chen carried out the quantitative analyses reported in this book. She was always sensitive to the substantive issues as well as keenly attentive to the technical details.

Several graduate students played a critical role on this project. Toni Terling, Ellen Slaten, and Patti Guiffre became fully involved in the interviews and provided insights into the bereavement experience. Anna Campbell and Sinikka Elliott worked tirelessly to iron out all the details.

Julia Hough of Cambridge University Press believes that the death of a parent truly is a turning point in adult development and I thank her for giving me the opportunity to explain how and why that turning point occurs. Thanks also to Kristen Wainwright and Heather Moehn of the Boston Literary Group for their advice and support and for introducing me to the wonderful Sharon Hogan.

I gratefully acknowledge the institutional support of the University of Texas for a research leave devoted to writing this book and to the National Institute on Aging for a five-year First Independent Research Support and Transition Award to study the effects of a parent's death on adult children (NIA R29 AGO8554). Thanks to Cecilia Dean and the Population Research Center at the University of Texas for administering and nurturing this project over the years.

Some of the ideas and findings reported in this book were first developed and published in academic journals. I appreciate the comments and scholarly advice from the editors and anonymous reviewers at the *American Sociological Review*, the *Journal of Marriage and the Family*, and the *Journal of Social and Personal Relationships*. Some of the findings on relationships with surviving parents were first presented in *The Parental Experience in Midlife*, edited by Carol Ryff and Mildred Seltzer (1996) of the University of Wisconsin.

I thank Sydney and Miriam Moss of the Philadelphia Geriatric Center for their warmth and for providing the first public forum for my findings on the effects of parent loss in their session at the Gerontological Society of America almost a decade ago. I am indebted to and inspired by my Austin circle of friends and, especially, my book group, for nurturing my multiple projects during the writing of this book.

Special thanks to Eliza, Aaron, Jordan, and Ruby for teaching me that there is more to family than writing about it and to Jordan for all the talking about writing.

As I wrote this book, I always thought of Eliza and Aaron. It is my greatest hope that I am giving them the love, strength, and confidence that they will need in order to parent themselves after I am gone. Except, of course, that I will never be truly gone – part of me will live on within my children, always there when they need me.

Ginger describes her father as a gregarious man, a man full of life. She was always close to him and recalls a childhood filled with happiness and love. As an adult, Ginger remained closely involved with her parents and was especially likely to turn to her father for advice. When Ginger's father died of a heart attack eleven months before our interview, she felt emotionally undone. She missed him profoundly and was worried about her seventy-two-year-old mother, who was devastated by the loss of her husband. In the midst of grief, Ginger was in a car accident and broke her back. At the same time, she was struggling in a marriage that left her feeling emotionally isolated.

   While the situation appeared bleak, Ginger was slowly undergoing a personal transformation that would turn her life around. This transformation was inspired by the death of her father, by the kind of person her father was, and by her past relationship with him. Ginger did a lot of thinking as she lay flat on her back in a hospital bed:

My father was always very enthusiastic. He did so much. He was always involved. He always felt that you can just sit around and watch other people have a good time or you can

1

do it yourself. . . . It just reminded me that, "Hey, life goes on honey." You can sit home and be miserable and get fat or you can do something. So I've lost thirty pounds since then. I really got control of my own life again. Control that I had given away for a while. My father's death was the catalyst that finally got me out of an unhealthy marriage.

Ginger, like many bereaved adults, experienced a turning point in her life and in her view of self after her father died. She is a changed person. She is more like the person she wants to be, and that makes her happy. The person she wants to be is very much shaped by who her father was. Ginger absorbed the parts of her father that she admired — healthy qualities of her father's that now live on in Ginger's personality. As she began to live life more fully, becoming more similar to her father, Ginger realized that her marriage did not allow her to be the person she wanted to be. As a result, Ginger divorced her husband. Leaving her husband meant abandoning parts of her personality that she did not admire and reclaiming parts of herself that were hidden and in need of acknowledgment.

In spite of the positive outcome, this has not been an easy time for Ginger. The divorce was difficult and she continues to deal with her mother's intense grief. Ginger's parents had a good marriage and her mother's loss is the most challenging aspect of coping with her father's death:

My mother was so devastated by it all. . . . She's still really grieving. And that was the most difficult for me – to see her grief. . . . This is something that I could not help her with and that hurt a lot.

Ginger now checks in on her mother almost daily and is more nurturing and protective of her. Ginger is experiencing some role reversal with her mother and feels "more the parent now than ever before." Taking care of a surviving parent can be very stressful for adults, but Ginger's newfound strength and renewed satisfaction with her life since her father's death ease the difficulty of caring for her mother. She explains, "My dad's death brought home to me that life is pretty short and you should spend the time with your family....Don't wait, don't put it off."

Embracing her father's personal qualities has made Ginger a happier and more confident person: "He's always a part of me. What he gave me and helped me develop into. There will always be that part of him in me."

1

ORDINARY LOSS, EXTRAORDINARY CHANGE

A myth supported by most theories of pre-adult development is that at the end of adolescence you get yourself together and, as a normal, mature adult, you enter into a relatively stable, integrated life pattern that can continue more or less indefinitely. This is a rather cruel illusion since it leads people in early adulthood to believe that they are, or should be, fully adult and settled, and that there are no more major crises or developmental changes ahead.

PSYCHOLOGIST DANIEL LEVINSON AND COLLEAGUES[1]

You can expect to feel terrible for a while.... You won't know what a parent's death is like until it happens to you.... It may be a common experience but common experiences can have profound effects. JAMES, AGE THIRTY-EIGHT

It was unusual for a middle-aged adult to have a living parent only a few decades ago. Today, it is common. In fact, parents are not expected to die until they reach old age; it is not unusual now for the lifespans of parents and children to overlap by a period of fifty years or more. At the same time, childhood has changed over time in Western cultures so that the period of our dependency on parents is longer than ever before. Thus it is often not until we begin, as adults, to confront our own aging at the same time that we experience the busiest years of our family lives and careers that a parent is likely to die.

Before we have experienced the death of a parent, we may expect that this will be a fairly minor milestone in our adult development. In fact, we may implicitly believe that once we reach adulthood, particularly if we have children of our own, that our development is more or less complete. We do not expect that there will be major changes in the way we experience the world or react to it. The research on which this book is based, however, demonstrates that the loss of a parent has profound and wide-ranging consequences for most of us.

Adults expect their parents to precede them in death, yet still the loss is jolting. Very few people who have not lost a parent anticipate the impact of this experience. Friends, coworkers, and even relatives often minimize the extent of loss felt by adults following a parent's death. Until recently, the popular perception has been that psychologically healthy adults who lose a parent do not suffer lasting psychological consequences. Friends and coworkers expect us to quickly recover, resume our usual social roles, and emerge largely unchanged shortly following such a loss. Some people presume that adults who are emotionally undone by a parent's death must have had emotional problems to begin with. The research presented in this book contradicts this view and shows that ordinary adults are strongly affected and changed by the loss of a parent.

The death of a parent is a turning point in the emotional, personal, and social lives of most adults – an event that initiates a period of substantial change and redirection in the way we view ourselves, our relationships to others, and our place in the world. In turn, change in the self has important consequences for change in the structure and dynamics of families. In Ginger's case, she made a conscious decision to become more like her admired father. This new view of herself as a happier and more confident person was incompatible with her marital persona; as a result, she divorced her husband. As many of the men and women who agreed to be interviewed about their experiences with a parent's death can attest, the consequences are both highly individual and far-reaching. An individual who feels liberated by the death of a parent, for example, may decide to get the divorce they had desired but avoided for fear of that parent's disapproval; this, in turn, disrupts family structures. In another case, after a family matriarch dies, an adult child may adopt the deceased mother's roles and responsibilities in order to create and maintain a newly structured extended family.

We are beginning to understand the extent to which a parent's death, even if it occurs during adulthood, affects adults' well-being. The death of a parent imposes an unexpected crisis for most healthy, well-functioning adults. This crisis can result in high levels of psychological distress, increased risk for depression, impaired physical health, or increased alcohol consumption. These effects go largely unrecognized by everyone except those going through the loss, and the bereaved often assume that they are unusual in their strong response to the loss. Most adults are surprised by the intensity and persistence of their reactions, and are thrown off balance when their distress fuels changes in their interpersonal relationships, behaviors, social roles, and even in the ways in which they view themselves.

A central message of this book is that it is quite normal for parental death to have profound effects on ordinary people. Stringent statistical tests of national survey data show that parental death adversely affects psychological well-being for most adults. Yet the form that the reaction to a parent's death takes is highly individualized. For a small but not insignificant group of individuals, the effect may even be more positive than negative. This usually occurs when adults lose an extremely critical or dysfunctional parent. This sort of loss can be freeing to an adult whose self-image was long undermined by the parent. But even when the effects are positive, individuals experience significant *change* following a parent's death. Clearly, no adult should realistically expect a parent's death to leave them unaltered.

The loss of a parent represents a rite of passage into a new adult identity. Most rites of passage involve formal rituals that mark the passages. Recognition of the steps bringing us nearer to our adulthood takes many forms, ranging from First Communion and Bar and Bat Mitzvah ceremonies to a legal change in one's rights and responsibilities: drinking, driving a car, registering with the Selective Service. We announce weddings, for instance, in the newspaper, hold bridal showers and bachelor parties, give gifts to outfit the newlyweds' new home, and may even mark our new status and how it affects our relationship with others by changing our name. We mark births with parties and gifts, and arrange leaves of absence from our jobs; we prepare physically and emotionally by attending childbirth preparation classes or reading several of hundreds of books on how having a child changes your life. The death of an adult's parent, however, is characterized by minimal public recognition. The only formal rite of passage is that associated with any death: typically a funeral, a memorial service, or a burial.

Informally, however, many important transitions occur. For example, bereaved adults experience a change in relationships with others, in psychological well-being, in health behaviors, and in the view of themselves as adults who are no longer children. Anthropologist Robbie Davis-Floyd argues that a chief characteristic of rites of passage is a "gradual psychological 'opening' . . . to profound interior change."[2] This "opening" characterizes adults as they make the final transition into adulthood. The death of a parent launches a period of self-reflection and the transformation of adult identity.

THE RESEARCH PROJECT

I became interested in parental death after several years of studying ongoing relationships between adult children and their parents. Once I began to talk about my interest in the impact of parental death, it seemed that whomever I talked with had a story to tell about their loss and its life-altering impact. My own mother once told me that she thinks about her mother every day even though her mother died nearly thirty years ago. She still considers how her mother might advise her when she makes important decisions or faces difficult times. Shortly after that conversation with my mother, she almost died during a surgical procedure. This personal experience forced me to think about what her death would mean to me. I searched the library for research on parental loss in adulthood and was surprised to find almost no information. Finally, I decided to conduct my own study on the effects of losing a parent. Now, after ten years and scores of discussions with adults who have lost their parents, I have clear evidence that a parent's death is a life-altering event for most adults.

This book is based on evidence from several different sources and combines different research methodologies. First, I investigated the general effects of a parent's death on physical and psychological health, as well as on certain types of relationships, using data from a large national survey of individuals in the United States. This type of statistical analysis provides information about the general effects of a parent's death on an adult's health, well-being, and relationships.[3] The overall survey was designed to focus on the link between social involvement and health. Relationships with parents were a significant component of the survey. Survey participants were interviewed in 1986, 1989, and 1994. Between 1986 and 1989, some 204 of the 3,614 individuals originally interviewed experienced the death of a parent. These unique data allowed me to look at individuals both before and after the death of their parent, as well as to compare their health and relationships with those of their nonbereaved peers. I also carried my analysis forward to the 1994 interview to determine whether the effects of parent death so apparent in 1989 persist over time. The national survey is demographically representative of adults in the general U.S. population, so the results about the effects of parental death from the survey are generalizable to adults in the United States.

The national data provide striking statistical evidence that a parent's death has substantial effects on ordinary individuals; however, they provide little insight into the social and psychological processes through which a parent's death affects physical and psychological health, relationships, and self-perceptions. I conducted in-depth interviews with seventy-three adults who had recently lost a parent in order to take a closer look at these processes.

I began the second phase of research by talking with a reporter from the local newspaper about my findings on parental death from the national survey. The reporter then wrote a story on parental death and mentioned that I would be continuing the study by conducting personal interviews with individuals who had lost a parent in the previous three years. My office phone number was included in the story. I hoped to interview about twenty-five people, so I decided to be available at my office the day the story appeared. It was a Sunday morning; two of my graduate students and I showed up armed with bagels and tall cups of coffee, half expecting to spend the morning just chatting and hoping for the phone to ring. Three hours later, we had the names of about 200 individuals who were willing to be interviewed. We hardly had time to collect names, numbers, and a bit of background information from each person before we had to stop to answer other phones. Many of the people who called in were relieved to know that they were not the only ones to be deeply affected by the loss of a parent. Over the next several weeks, I received about fifty more calls from individuals who finally got around to reading that Sunday's paper.

Of course, the type of person who volunteers to talk about an emotional topic such as parent loss might be more outgoing or distressed than the average bereaved person. In an effort to reduce this type of self-selection bias in our in-depth interview sample, we made an effort to interview a range of individuals, diverse with respect not only to their level of emotional distress but to their age, gender, race, and socioeconomic status. We also conducted a mail survey of 117 bereaved adults who called in but who were not interviewed in person.[4]

Combining qualitative and quantitative research methodologies in this way enhances our understanding of peoples' experiences, because each methodology bears certain strengths and limitations. Statistical analyses of data from the national survey, for example, can be used to determine whether adults who experienced a parent's death became more depressed over time than adults who did not have this experience. But numbers alone cannot fully convey the emotions and meanings underlying reactions to loss. Qualitative data, drawn from in-depth, personal interviews with the bereaved were needed to assess the subjective meanings and dynamic processes associated with the statistical patterns revealed in the national survey data, in other words, how the people interviewed actually feel about the death of their parent, and how the experience has changed their lives. The qualitative data were derived from careful analysis of detailed, in-depth descriptions of bereavement experiences that adults provided in their own words. These detailed descriptions provide insight into the underlying dynamics and processes that lead to increased levels of depression and personal change among the bereaved.

Throughout my research, I considered group differences in the response to parent loss. I analyzed data from the national survey to assess for gender, race, socioeconomic status, and age differences in the effects of a parent's death on individuals. Although gender differences in the experience of parent loss are a consistent theme throughout this book, the national data reveal that the effects of the loss on mental health, physical health, and relationships rarely differ on the basis of race, socioeconomic status, or the age of adults. Neither were group differences, outside of gender, apparent in my in-depth interviews with the bereaved. Although family culture and expressions of grief may vary across racial and ethnic groups, my study suggests that the experience of losing a parent is similar across racial and ethnic groups in the United States. Bill, an African American man, emphasizes just what the data suggest: that the response to parent loss does not much differ across racial groups:

> My wife says . . . I have never been a very communicative person. . . . But when I saw that article about your study I went ahead and called. I didn't know if it was going to be really helpful. I didn't know what the purpose of the study

was, but I did want someone to know that black people grieve just like anybody else. Even though I'm a man and I'm forty-four, I was very close to my mother and yes, I cried, and I still cry because I lost my mother.

Although I cannot say, definitively, that African Americans, white adults, and other racial and ethnic groups in the United States experience parent loss in similar ways, the evidence points strongly in that direction. What seems to be more important in shaping individual responses to parent loss, in addition to gender of the parent and adult child, is the adult's unique life history, a history that reflects a lifetime of interactions with the parent.

INDIVIDUALS AND BEREAVEMENT

Social scientists who rely heavily on numbers and averages in their research are sometimes apt to lose touch with the people they are studying. It is not so easy to lose touch with these human realities when one combines the sterile analyses of survey data with in-depth personal interviews, as I did in this study. When I interviewed each bereaved adult, a personal life story unfolded, a story that began with a young child and his or her relationship to a parent, a story that moved through a life course, with all of its ups and downs, a story that ended with the loss of a significant person. Some of these stories were warm, loving, and full of humor, while others were characterized by conflict, neglect, and emotional pain. As I listened, the adult in front of me was often transformed into a small child describing his or her childhood thoughts and feelings about a parent. It is to those young children and the adults within whom they reside that I owe this book and my own personal growth that resulted from this experience.

This book is intended for several audiences. First, this book is for individuals who are coping with the loss of their own parent or for those who have friends and loved ones who are coping with loss. This information may better equip the bereaved to recognize their own responses to a parent's death and why they are changing in particular ways. It may also serve as a guide to help individuals channel their distress and personal change in desired directions. This book is also designed for scholars of adult development and the life course, family relationships and relationship loss, and intergenerational relationships. For those who want a fuller understanding of how the research project and statistical procedures were handled, technical information about research procedures is in the appendix. This book is also for the physicians, therapists, clergy, and other professionals who are often called on to assist bereaved individuals in coping with loss. Although the death of a parent is similar in many respects to other significant losses, this loss is unique, particularly in its impact on the family and as a transitional event in adult development.

Finally, it is not only adults who care about their parents. Parents feel like parents no matter how old their children are. Several years ago, I received a letter from an eighty-six-year-old father who had just read an article about my research. His response was to worry about his "children"; he wrote, "I know [I will die] in a very short time, although I am OK now. . . . Do you have any suggestions?? I will leave a very large loving and caring family." I was moved by this father's concern about his adult children and I wrote to him right away. I hope that parents may find in this book some ways of preparing their adult children for this almost inevitable loss.

2

UNEXPECTED CRISIS

"Did you love your mother?" ...

"The easy answer is yes. But it's too easy just to say that when you're talking about your mother. It's so much more than love — it's, it's everything, isn't it?" ... *"When someone asks you where you come from, the answer is your mother."* ... *"When your mother's gone, you've lost your past. It's so much more than love. Even when there's no love, it's so much more than anything else in your life. I did love my mother, but I didn't know how much until she was gone."*

ANNA QUINDLEN, *ONE TRUE THING* [1]

It hurt so bad and I had nobody to talk to. People said, "Well, your folks died. Gee, I'm really sorry...that's tough," and patted me on the back. Well, they had no idea.

MICHAEL, AGE FORTY-ONE

The death of a parent is the most common cause of bereavement faced by adults in Western society. [2] Each year, about 5 percent of the U.S. population is faced with this experience. Only one in ten adults has lost a parent by age twenty-five, but by age fifty-four, 50 percent of adults have lost both parents, and by age sixty-two, 75 percent have lost both parents. [3] On average, about thirteen years separates the death of one parent from the other. Most commonly, the death of a father precedes the death of a mother, primarily because the life expectancy of men is about seven years shorter than the life expectancy of women and because women typically marry men older than themselves. A mother's death is most likely to occur when her adult children are between the ages of forty-five and sixty-four and a father's death is most likely to occur when his children are between the ages of thirty-five and fifty-four.

The timing of this loss, such that the death of a parent is most likely to occur during one's middle years, makes it especially likely to result in developmental change for the individual. We commonly assume that once we are grown, our personalities, attitudes, beliefs, and priorities will change little, if at all, during the remainder of our lives; once we reach adulthood, we are "done." Psychologists who study developmental changes over the entire course of our lives, however, view middle adulthood as a period of life in which individuals are likely to become more self-reflective.[4] Life course scholars Glen Elder and Angela O'Rand argue that when a significant event occurs during a particularly important phase of adulthood, its impact on individuals can be amplified.[5]

Even though personal goals, priorities, and one's sense of self are relatively stable in adulthood, one's basic life trajectory can be shaken by major life events.[6] Stress researchers Blair Wheaton and Ian Gotlib explain:

> A trajectory is a continuation of a direction. It is the inertia in our lives that results from the sum of the forces that propel us toward a destination. A turning point is a disruption in that trajectory, a deflection in the path.

Indeed, the essential characteristic of a turning point is that it changes the direction of a trajectory.[7]

Stress results when there is a mismatch between demands from the environment and the individual's ability to cope with those demands; the greater the mismatch, the greater the stress. Decades of research establish that stress adversely affects mental and physical health. Highly stressed individuals are more likely to experience depression and alcohol problems, coronary heart disease, cancer, poorer overall physical health, and increased risk for premature death.[8]

The evidence in this book shows that the death of a parent is a stressful life event in the adult life course, an event that disrupts life trajectories and has adverse effects on mental and physical health. Moreover, the loss of a parent initiates a rite of passage in adult identity, in part because it is stressful.[9] Many types of personal change following a parent's death reflect the bereaved adult's attempts to reduce feelings of loss, social and personal upheaval, and distress.

This loss also leads many people to reevaluate the self and relationships with others and to examine their personal priorities and goals in life. Pulitzer Prize–winning anthropologist Ernest Becker argues that obsessive denial of death is a defense mechanism adopted by individuals in order to protect themselves from an innate fear of death.[10] To this end, most people work, throughout life, to avoid thoughts of their own mortality. The death of a parent pierces this defense and confronts us with the reality of personal mortality. The death of a parent is more confrontational than other deaths because children so strongly identify with parents that witnessing a parent's death means witnessing the death of a part of oneself.

DIFFERENT WAYS OF EXPRESSING
EMOTIONAL UPSET

Stress exacts a psychological and physical toll from individuals, but everyone responds to stress in different ways. Some people become depressed. Others begin to drink heavily. Still others have headaches and stomach problems.[11] In my research, using national data, I looked at three common ways of expressing emotional upset and found that the death of a parent is associated with an increase in *psychological distress* and *alcohol consumption* as well as a decline in *physical health*.[12]

Psychological Distress

In scholarly and popular literature, bereavement is associated with feelings of despair and hopelessness, crying, troubled sleep, and diminished appetite. These are the classic symptoms of psychological distress and depression that psychologists see in individuals who have lost a spouse or a child. I find these same symptoms in adults who lose a parent. But grief and loss are much more than a list of symptoms. Each loss is a profound story for the bereaved person. In her novel, *Written on the Body*, Jeannette Winterson captures the unique poignancy attached to the loss of a loved person: " 'You'll get over it . . . ' It's the clichés that cause the trouble. To lose someone you love is to alter your life forever. You don't get over it because 'it' is the person you loved. The pain stops, there are new people, but the gap never closes. How could it?"[13]

I describe the symptoms of adults who lose a parent, but these symptoms have to be placed in the context of the bereaved person's social circumstances (what their life is about) and their life history (what their life has been like up to now). This context is what transforms a loss into a unique personal experience.

Throughout my interviews, I was struck by the differences in men's and women's descriptions and expressions of their grief. Of course, gender differences in emotional expression are not unique to parent loss. Throughout life, men and women are treated and socialized differently in ways that encourage emotional expression in women and discourage it in men. What may be unique to parent loss, particularly in response to mother loss, is the primitive childlike emotion, among women and men, that is tied to losing this primary connection to one's childhood. Certainly, strong emotion that comes from deep within may follow any significant loss, but the emotional response to losing a parent is rooted in early childhood when the fundamental attachment to the parent began. Fear of separation from the parent, loss of the parent, or abandonment by the parent are fundamental to early personality development; that this childhood fear ultimately becomes a reality evokes a response that reflects all of these early and symbolic associations with the parent.[14]

This fundamental sense of loss that adults feel after a parent dies may be similar for men and women, yet early experiences with parents contribute to gender differences in the experience and expression of that loss. Sociologist Nancy Chodorow emphasizes that the early socialization of children leads girls to have more permeable ego boundaries than boys in their relationships with others. Girls then are more likely to experience blurred boundaries between self and others, particularly between self and mother. Boys, on the other hand, are more likely to erect boundaries between self and other and, as a result, compartmentalize their social and emotional lives.[15] This tendency often leads men to use avoidance strategies to cope with the loss of a parent.

Compared with adults whose parents are alive, adults who lose a parent experience a significant increase in psychological distress symptoms, yet the reactions to loss, as well as feelings about those reactions, clearly differ for adult sons and daughters. Moreover, the gender of the parent matters. For example, increasing distress is seen following a mother's or a father's death, but the increase is somewhat larger following a mother's death.

Jonathon's mother died suddenly, at the age of seventy-two, from a heart attack. He describes the loss of a much-loved and very loving mother, a relationship of lifelong warmth:

> We were very close when I was a child. You know, I adored my mother as a little boy.... I can remember her kissing me goodnight and tucking me in.... The rest of my family would taunt me, saying I was a "mama's boy." It wasn't vicious taunting but part of our family romance.... I've lost the person who loved me and accepted me unquestionably and well, vice versa.

Like many of the men I talked with, Jonathon feels a profound sense of loss and emotional distress over his loss, but he works very hard to keep his emotions in check:

> I grin and bear it. Really, there's nothing you can do. It's outside of my control whether a depressed or empty feeling washes over me.... I've been tranquilizing myself for a long time anyway.... I have this dull feeling, this depressed feeling sometimes. Not such an unhappy feeling, but still a sadness.

We know from stress research that men are less likely than women to respond to stress with psychological distress symptoms, but even when men reported symptoms of psychological distress in my interviews with them, a clear gender difference emerged. Like Jonathon, many men felt compelled to bury and avoid their feelings.

Women are much more likely than men to fall into their grief, expressing their feelings of sadness through crying and talking about the loss with others. Yet both men and women talk about the relief they feel when they express their feelings. For example, Jonathon describes two "good cathartic breakdowns of shaking and crying" as therapeutic, although he quickly adds, "I don't expect that I'll have anything like that again":

> Just a good kind of letting go, a very relieving feeling. The first one . . . my sister asked me to water my mother's plants. My mother had a green thumb and there were a lot of plants. We both knew that those plants weren't ever going to get the care that they had had. And so I was out there watering the plants and I had found one that she had thrown out of the pot, out in the yard. So I got down on my knees scrambling around in the dirt [Jonathon holds back tears] and I repotted the plant and that's when I finally broke up and sat down on the bench and was shaking inside for several minutes and that was a great relief. . . . Normally I wouldn't allow myself to be physically overwhelmed like that. . . . I would be more stoical.

Women are more likely to talk freely about the need to express emotion and the psychological value in that expression. Not surprisingly, women were more likely than men to cry shortly following the loss as well as months and years later. Helen, fifty-two, describes her exhaustive crying following the death of her father:

Oh, I just cried and cried and cried and cried a lot. . . . I cried every day for thirty-five days. I just could not stop. I mean for hours during the day, I would cry. In my job I drive long distances, and I had a lot of time to cry in the car. It helped. . . . I could cry and think and, you know, talk to myself about things.

When I talked with men and women about the greatest sources of strain in dealing with their parent's death, I found another, parallel gender difference. Women were much more likely than men to describe, at great length, how their spouse or partner felt uncomfortable with their strong emotional reactions to the loss and, frequently, how their spouse had let them down emotionally during this time of need.

Lorrie's parents died within six months of one another almost three years ago. Lorrie, thirty-two, feels very close to her husband, but she was frustrated with the degree to which her husband was unable to cope with her emotion:

My husband has trouble demonstrating concern and affection. I've always known that but after the death I needed more comforting than he showed me.

Men, on the other hand, while appreciating emotional support from their partners, often want their partner to help them to ignore their pain. James's mother died two years before I interviewed him; James, thirty-eight, describes how he did not want his wife to respond to his feelings of depression:

> I felt trance-like. I had difficulty understanding things and stuff like that. . . . I lost concentration, being able to understand things. . . . I drank more too, that's for sure. I felt depressed for a long time. . . . When I'd get upset, my wife would be upset and she'd want me to feel better. But I don't know – it just didn't seem like anything helped me. Sometimes I just really didn't want anybody to help me or talk to me about anything.

Bobby, forty-one, tries to explain the need for men to be stoic in the face of emotional upset:

> It's the John Wayne syndrome. . . . Men just don't seek physical or mental health care as much as women. . . . I've cried around my son sometimes kind of purposely just to let him know it's okay. But, on the other hand, I haven't just really broken down because he would be worried. . . . In terms of emotionally expressing it, I have been pretty much keeping a lid on it.

Men are more likely than women to use avoidance strategies to cope with their feelings of upset, such as staying busy with work, exercising more than usual, or drinking. Women also use avoidance strategies, but women are more likely than men to alternate avoidance strategies with coping strategies that involve the expression of emotion.

Alcohol Consumption

The chief reason used by adults to explain drinking more following the loss is that alcohol numbs painful feelings and facilitates sleep, at least temporarily. Many of the people who drink more following a parent's death are people who drank heavily to begin with. This is the way that some men and women routinely cope with stress in their lives; when a parent dies, an existing pattern is exaggerated.

James's mother committed suicide at the age of fifty-eight. His mother had struggled with schizophrenia since James, now thirty-eight, was fifteen years old. James was close to his mother and understands why she killed herself. He describes himself before his mother's death as someone who drank "a lot," but after her suicide he began to drink more heavily:

> I drank more, that's for sure . . . probably thirty to fifty percent more than I did before, but it wasn't like I became an alcoholic or something, at least to my own estimation. . . . I really had – especially for the first six months – a real hard time just trying to feel normal. I felt not myself for a long time.

James, like many people in this study, feels that although the relief provided by alcohol is only temporary, it helps him avoid disturbing thoughts and feelings; alcohol helps him to feel "normal."

Decline in Physical Health

Adults who lose a father or a mother experience a greater decline in physical health over time compared with individuals who do not experience this loss. Many bereaved adults feel that the stress of dealing with the loss leads to their health problems. Lois, thirty-seven, describes how the death of her father affected her health:

> I worked. I didn't sleep. I never ate. I got down to eighty-six pounds. . . . I was breaking out in hives. I didn't weigh anything. I couldn't have lost another pound. I would have been in big trouble. . . . I was trying to do school and work and everything else and trying to do everything around the house.

Although the stress of bereavement often undermines physical health, some bereaved adults alter their health behaviors in ways that ultimately benefit their health. Many of the people I interviewed reported that they take better care of their health than they did prior to the loss. The national survey also reveals pockets of improvement in health behavior: For example, some individuals begin to drink less following a parent's death than they drank prior to the death. Why, during this time of loss, would an individual develop healthier behaviors? A parent's death differs from other stressful life events because the death itself highlights the adult child's own inevitable mortality. The bereaved are well aware that a parent's death may foreshadow their own future health risk and life span because of the strong genetic component in many diseases – for example, heart disease, diabetes, stroke, and certain types of cancer. This awareness can result in a change in behaviors that benefit one's health.

Tina, thirty-five, became more concerned about her own health after losing her mother to cancer and her father to a heart attack: "I think about my own health and I tell my husband, we're targets in our family. We've got cancer and heart disease in both of our families and we had better really take care of ourselves."

The effects of parent loss on physical health are very uniform across individuals, with generally adverse consequences. Yet we see that, for a significant number of individuals, some positive health consequences may occur in the longer run. As we see below in this chapter, positive change in health behavior is more likely among some groups than others.

IS MOTHER LOSS DIFFERENT FROM FATHER LOSS?

Certainly, research on parents and children might lead one to expect that adults would be more upset by a mother's death than a father's death. Children of all ages tend to be more involved with and feel closer to their mothers than their fathers. First and foremost, mothers play a more active role in parenting throughout the life course.[16] Mothers shoulder primary responsibility for infants and children even when employed outside the home. Mothers are more likely than fathers to provide physical care to infants and young children, such as changing their diapers and bathing and feeding them. Mothers also provide more emotional sustenance to growing children, tending to bedtime, illnesses, and scraped knees. The notion that a child in distress or discomfort will typically run first to his or her mother is not an unfounded stereotype, and individuals carry this history forward through the life course, so that the emotional attachment to a mother remains qualitatively different from that to a father.

Sociologists Alice and Peter Rossi find that, once children become adults, mothers are much more likely than fathers to arrange family get-togethers and to maintain contact with their adult children by phone, mail, and visits. In addition, adults' relationships with mothers are more likely to be characterized by shared values and views, closeness, and stability than are relationships with fathers.

This picture of parent-child relationships suggests that a mother's death would be more distressing than a father's death to adult children. However, the research evidence does not wholly bear this assumption out. When I look at alcohol consumption as a response to the loss, it seems that adults are more upset by the loss of a father, yet more psychological distress arises in response to the death of a mother. These effects mirror the kind of relationship that children tend to have with mothers and fathers. Relationships with mothers tend to be more psychologically nuanced and emotionally closer than relationships with fathers, perhaps making an emotional response more likely following the loss of the mother. Relationships with fathers, on the other hand, tend to be more emotionally distant, and more activity-focused; alcohol consumption is a less emotional and more behavioral response to loss.

PREDICTING PERSONAL VULNERABILITY TO PARENT LOSS

The gender of the bereaved adult shapes reactions to parent loss, but personal vulnerability to the loss is also influenced by whether it was a mother or father who died, what kind of mental and physical condition the parent was in before the death, and whether or not the parent exhibited dysfunctional behaviors dating back to the bereaved adult's childhood. Because the data support the idea that the risk factors for distress following a mother's death differ from those that follow a father's death, it is worth discussing these separately.

Risk Factors for Psychological Distress: Gender of Child and Impairment of Mother

Gender differences in response to a parent's death are exacerbated in cases of physical or mental impairment of the parent. As adults grow older, they are increasingly likely to have a physically or mentally impaired parent. Certainly, one would expect a parent's impairment to alter the nature of the parent–adult child relationship and influence the adult's response to the parent's eventual death. This does, in fact, occur, yet in different ways for sons and daughters. Among women, those who have a healthy mother who dies suddenly are most vulnerable to psychological distress. In contrast, among men, those whose mother is mentally or physically impaired at the time of her death experience more distress. This difference is not surprising when I look more closely at the family context. Whenever a mother is impaired, daughters are much more likely than sons to play an active role in caring for the mother's personal needs. Such caregiving is very stressful, and daughters find caregiving to be even more stressful than do sons. The death of an impaired parent may then mean a greater reduction in stress for caregiving daughters.

Jeannie, thirty-one, spent about a year caring for her mother before she died of cancer. Jeannie and her mother had always been close friends and they enjoyed shopping for antiques together. Jeannie experienced the chronic strain of providing care to her mother and felt relief following her mother's death:

> I did a lot of running errands ... getting medicine and booties, her shoes and wigs – it is kind of like I never got away even though I got away. . . . Those last two months were really hard because she suffered so. . . . I was getting

to the end of all my sick leave and I didn't know what I was going to do.... When she died, I almost felt guilty for feeling relieved but it was good at the same time. I was relieved also for me because there had been a lot of pressure. It was just a burden that was over my head. I thought about nothing else.

Since sons typically provide less care than daughters do to their impaired mothers, sons may feel some guilt following the loss of an impaired mother, and this guilt may translate into elevated distress levels. For instance, Bill, forty-four, remains distraught over the death of his mother, who died of cancer two years ago. Bill learned that his mother had cancer about six months before she died. He visited her twice, but regrets not making more of an effort to see and care for her. He describes his feelings shortly after his mother died:

A lot of guilt – about having always been so far away from home.... A lot of guilt over the fact that I was so far away from her. People say I should have done this and that, you know. Plus the fact that Mama always took care of all of us.

Sons may also be less prepared than daughters for the death of a mother who is impaired precisely because they are less involved in caring for her and are less aware of the extent of her decline. When a loved one experiences a long period of illness prior to death, the survivor has more time to prepare psychologically. During this time, the adult child engages in anticipatory coping: imagining what it will be like without the parent and how one will go about life in his or her absence. Anticipatory coping allows some of the grieving over a loved one to occur before the death.[17]

An extended period of caregiving, more common for daughters than sons, provides the opportunity for anticipatory coping. Terri, thirty-four, notes, "I felt like I had done a lot of grieving before she died because she was so ill."

Taking care of an impaired mother helps to prepare daughters for their mother's eventual death, but this kind of preparation comes at some cost. As the mother becomes increasingly impaired, the daughter gradually loses the relationship with the mother who once cared for the daughter.

Terri provided care to her sixty-eight-year-old mother, Judith, for over a year before Judith died of lung cancer. Terri had been close to her mother throughout life and now feels the loss of a close friend. Terri's father died when she was fourteen, yet Judith always managed to provide a secure and happy home for Terri and her sisters:

My mom was a typical stay-at-home mom of the sixties. She did not work outside the home but she volunteered in the school a lot. She was a scout leader. She liked to do arts and crafts so that was also something that we would do together. . . . I got my love of reading from her – because of watching her read. I would say that we had a close relationship. I knew I could count on her. You know [Terri begins to cry], for driving me to the store to get poster board at the last minute for a project or something like that at school.

Except for a brief period of conflict and rebellion during her teen years, Terri and Judith remained close throughout life:

I felt our relationship grow closer and, in some ways, we were more like peers or equals, because I could identify with some of her struggles more and try to see things from her viewpoint. After I had my children . . . I just realized that she had a lot of experience behind her and that was important. I remember her coming to help me when my daughter was born.

One of the greatest difficulties for Terri was seeing the relationship change as Judith became sicker and sicker:

I was used to my mom being somebody I could go to and tell whatever was going on and kind of use her as a sounding board. . . . As she became ill, I began to withhold information. . . . But, with her illness, it's like this big shadow that pervades everything, so you can't have the same intimacy. . . . But then there's another part of you that you still need your parent. . . . The relationship changes . . . it became more and more of me being the parent and her being the child. In the last few months my mom's cancer spread to her brain. . . . All of her thinking processes were affected. . . . All of that deteriorated day by day. So we did switch roles.

Although Terri experienced some relief at her mother's death, this feeling was mixed with the extreme loss she felt, and had been feeling, during the long illness. The time she spent caring for her mother helped the grieving process to begin, long before her mother's death.

Relief Following a Difficult Father's Death

Significant numbers of adults experience improved social and psychological functioning following a parent's death. This depends, to a great degree, on one's past, especially one's childhood experiences with the parent. Adults who grew up with an alcoholic parent may experience a reduction in psychological distress following that parent's death. This seems to be especially true after a father dies.[18] Many bereaved persons told me stories that support this interpretation.

Thinking of her childhood, Tina, thirty-five, describes her father as an extremely difficult man:

> He could get physically threatening. . . . There were times when he kind of pushed me around and . . . I thought he was being rough with Mom. . . . He had a really volatile temper – we had dents in the walls all through our house. There's a door to a bedroom that still sticks because he kicked the door in. . . . It wasn't like we had done anything to provoke the behavior. Sometimes, it was, "Get that look off your face," that sort of thing.

Tina's father continued to be difficult as he got older. Whenever he visited Tina or her siblings, he invariably disrupted family gatherings by disagreeing with someone over something. And he continued to treat Tina's mother badly. Her brother and sister refused to even see their father.

Initially, the death of Tina's father hit her hard, but now, eight months after the loss, she is doing well, even viewing life in a more positive way. Tina's improved outlook may have something to do with losing the responsibility of dealing with her father. Until he died, she was the child in the family who checked on him regularly, even though he was often rude and abusive when she did so.

Lois, thirty-seven, also had an extremely angry father and spent most of her adult life trying to create a better relationship with him. Lois's father was abusive and alcoholic when Lois was a child and spent little time with her as an adult:

> Well, there wasn't much of a relationship when I was a child...he was an alcoholic...there was no closeness growing up. I mean there was no closeness at all. I think as I got a little older...he drank all the time....He was real tough. I mean he was real tough. Real tough. It was actually a really abusive childhood....I just thought that was normal. But it wasn't.

Lois feels that her life has improved because of her father's death. She does not attribute her greater happiness to losing a difficult father. She believes that she is happier because his death gave her a better perspective on life: "I'm more aware of what's important." Lois acknowledges that she was the type of person who stayed busy especially when things were not going well, because staying busy is a way to avoid disturbing thoughts and feelings. Now that her father is gone, Lois does not feel the need to avoid her thoughts and feelings, which she feels is not a coincidence. When her father was alive, she felt a need to avoid strong emotions that, in relation to her father, felt as though they would have no limit. This frightening sensation has abated since her father died and she feels more in control of her emotions.

Sons and daughters are also differently affected by a father's death if, when growing up, their father had mental health problems. A daughter whose father had a mental health problem will tend to exhibit reduced distress following his death. This is similar to the relief effect that seems to occur after an alcoholic father dies. On the other hand, a bereaved son whose father had a mental health problem exhibits much more psychological distress than a bereaved son whose father did not have a mental health problem.

Vulnerable Men: The "Like Father, Like Son" Stress Response

Sons often respond to a father's death in a way that parallels how their father dealt with stress. Thus, a son who grew up with a father with mental health problems experiences more psychological distress than other adults in response to a father's death. Like their fathers, these sons exhibit psychological distress symptoms in response to stress. Likewise, a son whose father had an alcohol problem is more likely to increase his own alcohol consumption following his father's death: On average, an increase of about a hundred drinks more per month follows the father's death. On the other hand, sons who did not have an alcoholic father reduce their alcohol consumption by about twenty-nine drinks per month following the father's death. Daughters do not exhibit these patterns, perhaps because they identify less than sons with fathers, and as a result, they are less likely to respond to the father's death in a way that reflects the father's previous problems.

Several of the men I interviewed report strong similarities between themselves and their difficult fathers in ways that support the idea of a "like father, like son" stress response. For example, George, age fifty, grew up with a difficult and unloving father:

> When I was born, my father was in the Navy in World War II so we didn't meet until I was three and right after he came back my sister was born. . . . I think that he resented coming back and having a family and responsibility and that resentment was manifested in how he treated

me. . . . When he came back, I got asthma and I was real sick and I can remember him getting angry about me being sick.

George describes his father as an angry, violent, and unpredictable man. It is painful for George to recognize, but he sees his father in himself:

[George begins to cry softly.] I was thinking how much we were alike. . . . We look alike, we act alike. I can be impatient, explosive. There's a whole bunch of things that I try to work on that are like he was.

Identifying with the deceased father, keeping the father tucked within oneself, is a way for sons to keep the father alive. That some of the father's most salient characteristics were dysfunctional does not preclude their absorption into the son – particularly in a culture such as ours in which men receive the lifelong message that they are "their father's son," a "chip off the old block." In addition, sons may be unconsciously motivated to keep the father alive because the father's death means the end of any possibility for a relationship with a "good" father. This causes George considerable anguish:

I know that I'm still resentful of the way he treated me when I was young. I'm fifty years old. If this doesn't go away pretty soon, I'm going to see a professional about it. Especially since, you know, he's not here anymore. . . . He just didn't have the parenting skills, but even if I can figure out that stuff factually, it just doesn't make everything okay.

George's own history shapes not only his reaction to the loss of his father, but also his future social experiences and psychological functioning. As long as the father is available – even if he is available only within the son – the son has a chance of getting what he needs from the father. When asked if there was anything that made it easier to cope with the loss, George says:

> I don't look at it as final. . . . In my case, it was a negative relationship, but it's still the sense that it's not fully terminated. There's a possibility that it could lighten up a little.

By exhibiting the traits of his father, George has the opportunity to deal with his father's negative qualities. Although it would not be easy, if George could conquer those qualities in himself, perhaps he could begin to make peace with his father.

Adults like George are often surprised at the extent of their sadness following the loss of a parent they rarely saw before the death: "What I remember most was how sad I felt. . . . That's what surprised me about the whole thing is that I would even feel anything."

Some adults grieve especially hard following the death of a difficult parent, and they often have trouble understanding why they care so much. These adults hurt very much following the loss of a parent who they feel never loved them, was never proud of them, or was disappointed in them. And these feelings are more likely to occur when a childhood involved a violent, alcoholic, mentally disturbed, or neglectful parent. Even after the parent dies, these adults yearn for resolution.

In contrast to sons, daughters with negative childhood memories of fathers (e.g., memories of a father's mental health or alcohol problems) typically exhibit either no change or improved functioning following the father's death. Daughters may be less upset than sons when a troubled father dies because the death has a very different symbolic value for daughters. They may have been more likely than sons to perceive fathers with mental health or alcohol problems as threatening. Daughters are also more likely than sons to assume caregiving responsibility for impaired parents and to feel responsible for the well-being and problems of others. A lifelong sense of threat and responsibility may be burdensome, and, consequently, daughters may feel more relief than do sons when a troubled father dies.

Drinking Less After a Father Dies

On average, alcohol consumption increases following a parent's death, and this increase is more likely following a father's death than a mother's death. However, a closer look at social context shows that some people actually start drinking less following a father's death. Married persons and individuals under the age of forty-seven often reduce their usual alcohol intake when a father dies. Younger adults may reduce their alcohol consumption because they are more concerned about the implications of the parent's death for their own mortality. On average, younger adults have younger parents, and the experience of the premature death of a parent may be more likely to jolt younger adults into behaving in ways that protect their health.

Jody, at the age of twenty-seven, was young when her mother died prematurely of emphysema. Jody exemplifies young adults whose health behaviors improve following a parent's death. She is drinking less and exercising more, and she directly attributes these changes to her mother's death: "My mother smoked a lot, drank, and didn't take care of her body. I want to live a good healthy life and take care of my body so I will have good health later on in life."

Married adults may improve their health habits following parent loss for a different set of reasons. Married persons are much more likely than unmarried persons to report that someone tells or reminds them to do things to protect their health on a regular basis, and that someone is almost always their spouse.[19] Spouses are particularly likely to serve in this role if they perceive that their partner is vulnerable to a specific health risk (e.g., if there is a history of heart disease in the partner's family, the spouse more closely monitors the partner's diet and physical activity). Following the death of a father, the partners of bereaved adult children may become more concerned about the health of the bereaved person and play an even stronger regulatory role. For example, Lois's husband sent her roses and encouraged her to stop working so hard and take better care of herself. Lois's health had been compromised because she was so anxious and stressed following her father's death.

That married and younger individuals reduce the amount they drink following a father's death shows that a parent's death can result in positive behavior changes for some people. This is a very unusual response to a stressful life event. Most stressful life events contribute to negative health behaviors as individuals try to cope with the stress by smoking more, drinking more, and so on. The death of a parent is an unusual stressor in this regard because the parent's health and mortality has more potential to accurately portend the adult child's future health status. Following the death of a parent, adults may begin to think more seriously about their own mortality. Kim, thirty-three, drank heavily and overate following her father's death. She eventually realized that what she was doing could shorten her life:

> You wake up one morning going gosh, I'm going to kill myself doing this. You face your own mortality and you think, "This could happen to me. I'll be thirty-four years old in January and I think, you know, if I die as young as my parents did I don't have that much time."

Kim was very close to both parents, but especially to her father. Such emotional closeness in a relationship with a father can make an adult child feel loved and cared for, and this kind of supportive relationship benefits adult well-being. Yet losing an emotionally supportive father is a risk factor for bereaved adults. In comparison to those who received little emotional support from their fathers, such individuals substantially increase the amount they drink following the father's death. Similarly, a daughter who spent more time with her father prior to his death starts to drink more than a peer who saw her father less often – probably because she was closer to her father and feels a greater sense of loss after his death.

Kim remembers her father as one of her best friends and confidants. His death led to a tremendous increase in her drinking. Kim's mother died unexpectedly of a brain aneurysm just one year after her father died. Kim explained, "I lost my best friends, I lost my parents, I lost those people that I could turn to." She became depressed and drank heavily after each death, although she emphasized that she drank more following her father's death.

> For a period of time, I didn't want to eat and I couldn't sleep and you're depressed and you go through the usual things – not sleeping, not eating, and then after a while,

what I would do is go out and party with my friends. Go out after work, just go to the club and just sit and drink and drink too much and do that too often. I did that for about four months after each of them died. Usually during the summer months because I would start back to school in September and then I had to straighten up my act.

Kim felt that she drank more following her father's death, but ate more following her mother's death:

I did an awful lot of overeating when my mom passed away. I had two single friends, girlfriends, and what we would do is hit the clubs right after work and drink too much. Other nights we would get together at each other's houses and eat to the max. I would say that my alcohol consumption increased considerably after my dad died . . . it dulls the senses and it lulls you off to sleep, no matter how bad you feel the next morning at least you're sleeping and you can forget.

Kim's response to the death of her parents raises a fascinating and parallel possibility. Kim reports that she began to drink more in response to her father's death, but she overate in response to her mother's death. Certainly, in most families, mothers do most of the food preparation – on a daily basis and for special occasions – and food is associated with nourishment and comfort. In Ruth Gruber's book, *Haven*, she describes an encounter between herself and her mother that occurred just before Ruth left on a potentially dangerous mission to escort a thousand refugees from Italy to the United States during World War II. In this encounter Ruth's mother delivers a bag filled with homemade foods, and

Ruth makes the link between food and her mother: "Food, second only to her husband and her five children, was intimacy; food was survival; food was the tribal memory of all the countries Jews had wandered through. Food, she was convinced, Jewish food, kept the family together."[20]

Because of the strong emotional link between mothers and comfort food, adults may be more likely to turn to food for consolation following a mother's death than they would following a father's death.

The Importance of Resolution: Repairing a Life History

Unresolved issues with parents complicate recovery from the loss of a parent. Some adults spend most of their lives yearning for a different kind of parent: a more loving, less critical, or more stable parent. For most adults, the death of the parent only intensifies this yearning.

Diane, forty-six, is a schoolteacher and a happily married mother with two well-adjusted teenage children. She invited me into her warm and inviting home for our interview. Yet just beneath the surface of this charming and nurturing woman's smile is a deep-seated pain that she cannot escape, a pain stemming from a lifetime of hoping for a different kind of father.

Diane described her father as "larger than life . . . outgoing, talkative, and knowledgeable . . . he'd hold court in some ways. . . . I admired him greatly. I know that other people did. I would watch him entertain other people." But her father had a dark side. He was an alcoholic, never displayed any pride in any of his five daughters, and was often violent. Diane certainly feared her father when she was young. As an adult, he had little to do with Diane unless he was drunk. Diane's father would often call her late at night and rage on about whatever was currently on his mind:

> My father would call me on the phone late at night when he'd been drinking. He would start talking and my mother would get on the extension and they would get into this horrendous fight, then they'd hang up. I would wake my husband up and say, "They are going to kill each other." My husband would say, "What can you do? They've probably gone to sleep. . . . Forget it." And that is exactly what would happen. . . . I allowed this to go on. I would say, "Dad, I am awake during the day. Can you call me during the day? . . . I have to work tomorrow. I am tired." He would just go on like I had never said anything.

Her father's late-night calls included personal attacks on Diane and her sisters: "He started attacking all of our husbands. He said . . . all of you married wimpy men, passive men. . . . He would just put us down."

Diane never refused these calls from her drunken father. She describes herself as the good daughter who was always there for her parents. She desperately wanted to win her father's love and approval. Much of the anguish that she feels now is tied to never having had a loving relationship with her father:

> My father never said things like "I love you." . . . I can't tell you how many times I have hung up the phone and the kids would be here, my son and daughter, and I'd say, "I love you, Dad" and I would hang up and then I would say, "I love you too, Diane." The kids would laugh and say, "Oh,

Mom, give it up. It doesn't matter." I guess it doesn't. But just to have him say, "I am proud of what you've done." . . . I had . . . phony little ideas that, at some point, my father was suddenly going to turn and say, "You are a wonderful child." It was sad that things did not work out. . . . It was never going to happen. . . . There is no resolution, ever.

The distress associated with the inability to resolve a troubled mother/daughter relationship also resurfaced throughout my interviews with bereaved daughters. Stephanie, for instance, had a tumultuous relationship with her mother throughout life. Her mother was married five times and divorced four times. She divorced Stephanie's father when Stephanie was only two. Stephanie never knew her father and had strained relationships with several of her mother's husbands. Her mother drank heavily and was largely out of Stephanie's life. Stephanie, thirty-one, describes her final year of high school:

She started seeing this married man when I was a junior in high school. When I was a senior he left his wife and got an apartment. My mom basically moved in with him. She'd come home once a week and leave me money, you know, for groceries, and did laundry, made sure I was all right and stuff and then go back to him. . . . I was real bitter about that for a while.

Throughout childhood, Stephanie's mother could not be relied on as a parent, yet as an adult, Stephanie developed a sense of closeness to her mother. This is extraordinarily important to Stephanie, especially because she did not have a sense of security and stability as a child. Stephanie was only thirty when her mother died suddenly, of a brain aneurysm, at the age of fifty-two. Stephanie had never fully resolved her feelings of insecurity and disappointment with her mother and is now extremely distressed by her mother's death:

> When she died, it was like I didn't care. So I started smoking again and, right after she died when I was working first shift at work, I was drinking a lot. I'd come home from work and just drink until I would just pass out.

Stephanie desperately needed to know that her mother was there for her, a need made more poignant by her difficult childhood. She had established a fragile semblance of closeness to her mother and that is now lost. Stephanie, like many bereaved adults, says she still talks to her mother and feels her presence. Thus Stephanie holds on to the relationship and avoids the reality that complete resolution is beyond her grasp.

The pain of unresolved yearning for a certain kind of parent resounded through my interviews with bereaved adults. Yet it seems that those who manage to create a sense of resolution following the loss are often transformed in positive and adaptive ways. Paradoxically, this sense of resolution need not be deep, sincere, or profound in any objective sense.

Lois had had a difficult relationship with her father throughout life. Yet she feels that she grew close to her father and resolved lifelong issues in the two weeks prior to his death. After her father had a near-death experience, he opened up to Lois:

> He told me his whole life story. And he told me that he'd made mistakes as a child and he realized that and that

it was important to be happy and that we're all here for a reason. . . . That's when I finally got close to him. . . . I realized when he knew he was dying that he had a whole different outlook. I mean, there was no alcohol left in him. I know that. . . . He was a real macho type of man and the tears were rolling down his face. . . . After he died I realized how much that meant to me and how it brought us a lot closer. . . . It made the whole process easier. . . . Some people don't get that opportunity. . . . He told me, "We're all put here for a reason on this earth. I was put on this earth to have four wonderful daughters." And I had never heard that before out of him. And it was sad that it took that, to know that he was dying, for him to say it, but that's what it took.

Lois believes that it would have been a lot harder for her if her father had died unexpectedly. "I would have been a basket case. . . . People that have built up grudges or resentment – that would be the toughest part." This simple gesture from her father made up for a lifetime of abuse:

I had the opportunity to get closer to him and I never had been close before. I can almost forget a lot of the horrible things as a child because I have one good memory; that makes it a little bit easier.

This feeling of resolution often sets apart the adults who experience improved well-being from those with a similarly difficult life history who become more distressed following the death of their parent.

CONCLUSION

Any significant loss may result in distress and change for an individual, but the loss of a parent is unique in its ability to mark a turning point in adulthood that can propel significant change in adults. The relationship with a parent and the loss of a parent are unique from other experiences of loss in two fundamental ways. First, parents play a powerful role in creating the child's life history and establishing the foundation from which they experience the world and develop other relationships.[21] Second, adults remain children themselves until their parents die, at which point they must redefine themselves as full-fledged adults. In Nick Hornby's novel, *High Fidelity*, Rob rebels against the demands of adulthood, but he speculates about how a father's death might finally make a person into an adult: "We talk about her dad, mostly, or rather, what life will be like without him. And then we talk about what life will be like generally without dads, and whether it's the thing that makes you feel grown-up, finally."[22]

The process of ending one phase of life – being a child with living parents – and starting a new one – becoming a motherless or fatherless adult – engenders emotional upheaval for most people.

Personal changes that follow a parent's death are motivated by a need to reduce the feelings of loss and upset that follow a parent's death. The bereaved adult's social circumstances (past and present) as well as a lifetime of interactions with the parent shape the degree and direction of personal transformation.

A life history characterized by unresolved issues with the deceased parent is an important source of emotional upheaval following the loss. This is particularly the case where parents had lifelong behavioral, psychological, or substance abuse problems but also occurs in cases in which parents never provided any outward expression of love for or pride in the child. In families in which the parent managed to mend some fences in the years preceding his or her death, adult children often benefit greatly. Some adults benefit from parental apologies and expressions of caring in the weeks, days, or even hours preceding the death.

Although many adults who had a difficult childhood manage to create a degree of resolution with the parent at some point in adulthood, the past relationship may never be fully repaired. A childhood spent with an emotionally disturbed, abusive, alcoholic, or neglectful parent is a legacy that often endures beyond the death of the parent. Throughout life, most adults who suffered a painful childhood work to resolve their feelings of rejection, loneliness, and unworthiness. Losing the parent who created those feelings can contribute to emotional distress because losing that parent means losing the opportunity for the parent to repair the damage and to become the parent the child has always needed and desired. In a sense, life, for these adults, feels like it has a hole in it because the adult was never able to accomplish or obtain what is perceived as a critical part of the experience of being a loved child.

In contrast, some adults who had a difficult family history actually experience improved psychological functioning after the parent dies. In such cases, the death of a parent typically comes as a relief. This relief is especially apparent for daughters whose fathers had alcohol or mental health problems. Many of these daughters felt a sense of burden and responsibility for their father throughout life, a responsibility that dissipates after the father dies.

Mother Loss and Father Loss

I have suggested that adults respond to a mother's and father's death in ways that reflect lifelong differences in typical relationships with mothers and fathers. Relationships with mothers are more likely to have been characterized by emotional closeness, and adults are more likely to respond to mother loss with emotional upset. Relationships with fathers are more likely to have been characterized by instrumental activities (from play in childhood to watching television together in adulthood), and adults are more likely to respond to father loss with a behavior: alcohol consumption.

Change in the Self

The mental and physical health consequences of parent loss provide the first glimpse of personal change that follows a parent's death. Sons often become more like their fathers following the loss; for example, sons whose fathers did not abuse alcohol actually reduce the amount they drink, whereas sons whose fathers did drink increase their drinking. Daughters often feel liberated by the loss of a difficult father, and this sense of liberation may actually improve their psychological well-being. The loss of a difficult parent may free individuals to feel more comfortable about who they are and what they do. A parent's death can initiate change in one's perception of the inevitability of personal mortality. This changing view of self can affect personal health habits and lifestyles. These are only a few facets of fundamental change in the self that follow a parent's death. The following chapters show that these changes contribute to a transformation in adult identity.

3

SYMBOLIC LOSS

My father was probably the greatest single influence on me ever — of anybody. He was a role model, an adviser, an ... emotional anchor.
TOM, AGE FORTY-FOUR

Daddy, I have had to kill you.
You died before I had time —
Marble-heavy, a bag full of God,
Ghastly statue with one gray toe
Big as a Frisco seal
FROM THE POEM, DADDY, BY SYLVIA PLATH[1]

W hen a mother or father dies, an adult loses not only their parent, but also the abstract meanings associated with that parent. A mother or father may symbolize an all-powerful figure: the person who shaped the child's personality, the arbiter of rewards and punishments, and a key person for the child to emulate, to please, and to displease. This symbolic figure is both the elderly parent who dies and the many other versions of the parent that the bereaved individual has known from infancy to adulthood. When a parent dies, the adult loses a connection to the past that dates to the beginning of life. The parent's death also portends one's own mortality in a way that no other death can; in essence, the adult child joins the next generation in line for death.

A lifetime of interactions between a parent and child imbues their relationship with unique meaning. Parents arguably put more effort into defining and shaping an individual's identity than any other person does, and an individual's self-concept is formed, in part, as a reflection of the positive and negative aspects of this relationship.[2] Parents continue to affect the child's definition of self throughout the child's life; their influence never fully ceases and can never be fully erased. Adults carry this influence within themselves even if they want to escape it; psychotherapists devote considerable energy, and face tremendous hurdles, in overturning patients' early "scripts" with parents. Even in the parent's physical absence, internal dialogues with parents often influence adults' views of self. Many of us have experienced those moments of self-doubt when a parent's old admonitions suddenly appear in our thoughts. These internal conversations with parents can be very powerful, and they may trip us into "cycles of self-devaluation."[3] Of course, internal dialogues, if based on prior positive interactions with parents, may elicit cycles of self-affirmation and worth. We may continue to consider our parent's opinion and view the parent as a credible source of information about ourselves throughout life.

When a parent dies, the loss of this source of self-definition can challenge an adult's psychological well-being and lead to a redefinition of the self. Adults often look to their parents for validation of their value system, so the parent's death may cause them to question whether who they are and the attributes they possess are still worthwhile. For example, a man may not have achieved success in his career, but his mother may have convinced him that success was not all that important in light of his other qualities (such as modesty, consideration for others, or selflessness). With the loss of his mother, the affirmation of his self-identity may be shaken. Conversely, a man whose mother had always viewed him as a failure may begin to question this view of himself after his mother dies.

Our symbolic images of a mother and father are rooted in childhood and reinforced and reshaped throughout life. When bereaved adults talked with me about their parents, several symbolic images of parents emerged repeatedly. Some of these images are largely positive (e.g., parent as friend), whereas others are negative (e.g., parent as critic). Some symbolic images are more likely to contribute to adults' growth or transformation following the loss; other images contribute to a sense of psychological relief or continuing torment following the parent's death. Symbolic images of a parent thus are tied to the degree of emotional and psychological upset experienced during the period of bereavement, and they drive the specific arenas of personal change that any particular individual is likely to experience.[4]

POSITIVE IMAGES OF PARENTS

When the parent-child relationship is a positive one, the parent's death can represent the loss of the unique love that only a parent can offer a child, the feeling that the parent was always there if the child was in need. The death robs the adult child of a connection with the past, with childhood, and with someone who knew him or her since birth. The adult may also grieve the loss of a friendship, a sense of family, stability, a connection among generations of family members, the availability of a trusted mentor, and personal validation.

Friendship

Adults who think of their parents as close friends often describe a lifelong, emotionally supportive relationship in which they could be honest and open. In my interviews with adults, sons were more likely than daughters to view their lost fathers as friends while daughters were more likely to think of their lost mothers as close friends.

Jen, fifty-two, described her mother as the most supportive person in her life. Jen provided physical care for her mother almost around the clock in the four months before her death, and although her mother was incapacitated near the end, Jen remembers her mother as a close friend and confidant even during that time:

> I lost my best friend, my counselor, the person who never criticized me no matter what dumb thing I did, she just kept encouraging me. The person I could confide in and depend on in any situation. . . . Most importantly, I just don't have anyone I can share my life with – the ups and downs. She was so interested in everything I did. She loved to hear about my career and the things I was involved in and there is just no one that interested anymore.

Jen has two adult sons and she has been married for more than thirty-two years, but these relationships do not have the sharing, supportive, and unconditional quality of the relationship with her mother. In response to the loss of her mother, Jen has changed how she interacts with her adult sons: She now discourages their dependence on her because she does not want her own death to be too devastating for them.

Adults who were especially reliant on a parent for emotional solace or who feel that no one can ever love them as much as their parent did are at particular risk for psychological distress following parent loss. In Jen's case, she said that "for months after her death, [she] would wake up in the morning and think, 'What is the point?'" Adults who have looked to a parent to provide unconditional love tend to be more depressed and feel less recovered following the parent's death than do other bereaved individuals.

A Sense of Family

While some parents primarily represent friendship, other parents are more likely to symbolize the structure and emotional glue that defines the family. Kim fondly recalls that holiday dinners used to involve as many as seventy members of her extended family and that her parents assumed primary responsibility for these gatherings. She now feels the loss of a cohesive extended family as well as the loss of her parents:

> Holidays, the meals were always fixed at my parents' house. My mom and my dad would always host the dinners. When they were dead, it kind of fell apart and there was no real organization to it. My mom called everybody before the holidays – this is what we're having and this is when we're going to start dinner. . . . Everybody just showed up. . . . [We] don't have a nucleus [anymore].

Jen similarly describes how her family began to disintegrate after her mother's death:

> I feel I have lost my roots as my sister and I are not close and we don't have a very big family. All the holiday activities center[ed] on [my mother's] house and everyone in the family looked to her to organize whatever we needed.

The social, psychological, and even physical sense of family is altered by the loss of a parent, and the disappearance of a family or a family home is a tangible loss with important symbolism. Michael, forty-one, saw his family home as the emblem of family safety, security, and love:

> Taking their things off the walls that had hung there since I was a year old ... opening every drawer and finding another box of pictures. That in itself was part of the grieving process ... going through all that stuff and just taking my mother's life apart was extremely horrible ... emptying this house that was my whole life growing up. They lived at twenty-three twenty-one Kerbey Lane and I don't care what happened to you, if you could just make it to twenty-three twenty-one Kerbey Lane, you were OK, there was security there.

Adults who associate loss with "family" often seek to recreate the old family structure and essence. This often means taking on new roles within the extended family. In some cases, the death of a parent leads to a reconstitution of family, with increasing closeness among siblings and the emergence of a new matriarch or patriarch. These family changes are almost always viewed as positive. Lynn is surprised and pleased to find that all of her siblings began to feel closer to one another following her mother's death five months ago. She is partly responsible for this positive change because she has adopted her mother's central role in the family:

> I feel somewhat of a responsibility toward my brother and sister. . . . Somebody needs to keep the family together as a cohesive unit, to do the things my mother used to do. She would always communicate, let us know what the others were doing, and now I feel like we need to communicate with each other.

When an adult is unable to establish or restructure desired family ties, the sense of loss can be especially poignant. Jeannie, thirty-one, was extremely close to her mother. Jeannie and her father provided care for her mother in the months leading to her death from cancer. She now feels that her family is falling apart; she is estranged from her sister and her father recently asked her to stop visiting on Sundays because he is now dating someone:

> Mother's Day was hard and I just pretended that it was not Mother's Day. I did not go to church. I did not want to hear anything about moms and I guess that sort of started it. . . . Then by July fourth everybody was doing picnics and family hamburger outings and I thought I did not have any family. My dad was out of town a lot. He started seeing this other lady and I felt like I had no family. He was gone. He was gone for Mother's Day.

Family rifts can become more salient once a parent dies, and the bereaved adult may reevaluate the meaning and value of family, with its deficiencies and strengths. These reflections can affect the adult's sense of self by changing his or her priorities and outlook on life. The loss of her mother and the family that she once knew has sharpened Jeannie's sense of the importance of family and made her more focused on starting her own family – on getting married and having children right away.

In my discussions with the bereaved, women were more likely than men to associate the loss of their parent with the loss of family, and this tendency seemed to be even more likely in response to a mother's death. This disparity reflects gendered social contexts and women's greater involvement in family maintenance and concerns as well as women's generally closer relationship to mothers than fathers. Compared with men, women are more likely to organize family activities, keep family members in touch with one another, and provide care to sick and disabled family members. It follows then that women would be more likely to associate a parent's death with family change.

Individuals who feel a strong loss of family experience more emotional upset than other bereaved adults, perhaps because these adults were more reliant on the parent for a sense of family. Throughout my research, I saw repeatedly how the death of a parent leads to new family roles that are closely tied to a change in adult children's self-perceptions and identities. We explore pervasive changes in particular family relationships – with spouses, children, siblings, and surviving parents – in later chapters. Clearly, the restructuring of families and restructuring of self often go hand in hand.

Stability

While some adult children are particularly affected by the loss of a family center that their parent represented for them, others are left feeling off-balance by a parent's death because they looked to their mother or father for a sense of security and stability.

Hannah, thirty-two, grew up in a large and very close family, and she describes this closeness as being central to her family's culture and identity. Nevertheless, Hannah's family had its share of difficulties. In particular, her mother suffered from serious clinical depression and suicidal tendencies for much of Hannah's childhood. Her father, who died recently, managed to keep the family afloat through the many years of her mother's mental illness, and Hannah now strongly associates the memory of her father with a sense of security and stability:

> His number-one priority was his family under any circumstances. He was extremely loyal to his family, his wife, his business, his country, to everything. . . . I was actually much closer to my mother . . . but in terms of being able to count on my father always being there and being able to discuss anything – he was there a hundred and ten percent for as long as I can remember. . . . My mother was on a series of very strong antidepressants and psychoactive drugs for a decade and this made for many difficult years in our family, so my father had to act not only as a father but also as mother and he almost raised us single-handedly. . . . What have I lost? It is the Rock of Gibraltar.

Unmarried adults were more likely than married adults to associate the image of stability with a parent. Since a spouse is often viewed as a source of stability for the married, parents may be more likely to represent home base for the unmarried – a safe and affirming place that the adult knows is there, even if they do not need or use it.

Connections Across Generations

Adults who are parents themselves often mention their regret over the loss of a grandparent for their children. This loss is multidimensional: The grandchild loses the unique relationship offered by the grandparent, the grandparent loses the opportunity to enjoy the grandchild, and the adult child loses the pride and enjoyment of witnessing the relationship between grandparent and grandchild. When the parent dies, the sense of loss often is tempered by *generativity*, by the belief that the parent lives on in the child and in the grandchild. Generativity also relates to the connection between generations; it refers to the feeling that one is passing along a legacy to one's children, a legacy that was passed to the adult from his or her parents.[5] In fact, adults who have children of their own are more likely than childless adults to associate the death of a parent with generativity.

Alejandro never knew his own grandparents; Alejandro's parents left Cuba, and their families, to come to the United States in the 1960s. Alejandro admired his father very much for the sacrifices he made in coming to the United States and in supporting and educating his six children. In most respects, their relationship was formal and distant; in fact, Alejandro's father rarely touched Alejandro when he was a child. Alejandro's father died just a few weeks after the birth of Alejandro's first child, Francisco. Alejandro grieves for the loss of a grandfather for his son: "My son won't be able to know his grandfather and what a good man he was. . . . That really is the thing that I miss the most and that really hurt me when my dad passed away." Yet just before he died, Alejandro's father was able to meet Francisco:

> My dad was really hurting in those last months. Francisco was born on November fifth and my dad died December fifth. He told the doctors the whole time that he was not going to die until he saw his grandson. We had to wait three weeks until we could take him because of the baby's immunities. . . . It was hard because I was thinking the whole time, "Well, I sure hope he's not going to die before he sees him." We took Francisco down there and my dad saw him and recognized him. . . . He told us, "Just take care of him and love him and I'm really proud of you all" and he lost consciousness after that. The next week he told his doctors that he could die now since he saw his grandson.

Alejandro is now comforted by the connection between himself and his father and between his father and his son. Alejandro feels that he gave his father a precious and invaluable gift that reflects the respect he feels for his father. The generations are forever linked in Alejandro's mind.

Some adults become emotionally close to their parent only after having children of their own. Todd, forty-six, and his father had a tense relationship until Todd was in his forties and had a son:

> We were distant. He's a retired army officer. . . . Our ideas did not always agree with each other. There were a lot of conflicts because of that. . . . It was difficult for my father that I wasn't . . . doing the things that he wanted me to

do. . . . I didn't get married until I was almost thirty-
five. . . . I think that bothered him. After my mother died,
my father and I became closer just out of necessity. And
once I had my son, my dad just idolized Timothy. It was
reciprocal too. And so that brought us closer.

Todd's father called Timothy every night to say goodnight. Once
a week, Todd's father picked up Timothy from daycare and took
care of him for the evening. Todd's ability to share stories of his
father with Timothy is now a great comfort to him.

Generativity also involves the passing along of legacies from
one generation to the next. This may be expressed through documentation of a family's history. If their parent had historical
information that no one else knew about, the adult may feel a loss
of family history as well as the loss of a parent. Others are pleased
that their parent documented and left behind family records. Even
those adults who feel the loss of family history often focus on the
wealth of information that their parent possessed – there is the
warm belief that the parent knew something special and important and that any part of that history that can be maintained and
passed to the future is of value.

Jonathon, forty-five, especially appreciates the "intellectual
heritage" that he received from his mother, who was a medical
illustrator. Now, during his intense period of loss, compiling his
mother's artwork comforts Jonathon:

Going through her things is helpful because it's almost
like a reconstruction of the person. In a way, she lives
through her things. . . . They're representative of her and
so they are kind of imbued with her spirit. . . . So I'm in
the process of seeing if there is an archive of this kind

of material because I think this stuff is important.... It's helpful. It's keeping the link with her.

Generativity is also related to the symbolic loss of youth and the transition to adulthood that many adults feel when a parent dies. That is, the parent represents the older, adult generation; when the parent dies, the child assumes this position. The adult self is updated so that the adult becomes his or her own parent. Todd explains:

> I lost my childhood. All of a sudden I'm the father. I'm the head of the family.... That's a strange feeling. You know, there have been a lot of things written about members of my generation and about how we have a reluctance to let go of our youth. And I don't think I have a Peter Pan syndrome as it were, but... my wearing jeans, my long hair... all that bothered my father. He would make comments about how I don't act like an adult.... Well, now I am an adult because there's nobody else. My parents are both gone and there's nobody else. So I am the head of the family. I am doing all these things that he did.

In Todd's case, he began to actively cultivate his father's characteristics in himself so that personal change was very much directed by who his father was.

Certainly, individuals with children have, in their children, a reminder of the lasting links among generations. Experiencing those links may help to mitigate depression: It can give the loss positive meaning or even reduce the sense of loss – because the parent lives on through grandchildren or through the maintenance of family history. Embracing the continuity of life seems to be an adaptive response in coping with parent loss.

The Availability of a Trusted Mentor

While some bereaved individuals miss the friendship, family center, stability, or generativity that their parents represented, others view their parent as their most important mentor, teacher, or guide in life. The child may not miss the actual advice received, but simply the belief that it could be obtained if needed.

Warren, twenty-eight, remembers his father as a teacher even from childhood:

> When I was little, he read to me the Hardy Boys novels. . . .
> I lived out on a farm so it's not like I could ride my bicycle
> to a friend's house. So my dad and my mom and my dog
> were my world. . . . I was into being a little scientist with
> chemistry sets and microscopes and all that. My dad loved
> that part and so he just did everything he could to facilitate
> me learning and having knowledge about everything.

Warren describes his father's role as a mentor:

> He was to me a person who – whenever I had a problem,
> even through the teen years – would sit back and evaluate
> the problem as if he was not my parent and plot a solution
> for me . . . like a strict confidant. . . . I lost an information
> source . . . somebody who I saw as having the supreme
> amount of knowledge. . . . My mom loves me but she can't
> help me. . . . Whereas my dad would give me specifics to
> do. It's kind of like telling somebody they need to tie their

shoes but not showing them how. That's how my mom is. My dad would have shown me how to do it.

Warren misses having his father to guide him through life. Even as he succeeds and thinks his father would be proud of his accomplishments, he wishes that his father could see his successes and comment on the best way to proceed:

> I would give almost everything to have fifteen more minutes with him. . . . I just wish he was there for a short period of time just so I could bounce everything off of him that I've done and for him to see the things that I have done. . . . I just want for him to be proud of me. . . . My mom feels proud of me but she's limited in her knowledge of these things.

Personal Validation

Many children continue, through adulthood, to consider their parent as a positive source of information about the self. Parents may validate their adult children by continuing to provide unconditional love and personal affirmation.

Rebecca, forty-one, grew up in a strict Pentecostal family in which she was the youngest of eight children. Her mother was the disciplinarian; her father was the protector whom she describes as her "fortress." Rebecca feels that the essence of loss after her father's death was the loss of unconditional love:

> As long as your parents are alive it doesn't matter how old you are or what circumstances you're in, you always know that there is somebody alive on earth that it won't matter

what you've done, what you've experienced, what you've been through, what you're feeling. You always know that they are there with their arms open. And that's what I miss the most. . . . I know my daughter loves me that way. But that's a different kind of relationship.

Adults may miss their parents' affirmation of who they are and what they have accomplished. Claire, forty-one, lost both of her parents two years ago. When Claire was a teenager, her mother had a serious drinking problem that kept the family in turmoil for many years. When Claire became an adult, her mother quit drinking and she and Claire grew close to one another. She was fortunate in that she was able to achieve some resolution of her childhood yearning for a loving mother before her mother's death. In her later years, Claire's mother became an important source of personal validation for Claire:

My mother was always so supportive of everything I did. . . . I miss that support. . . . I really miss her more than I miss [my father], even though I thought I would miss him a lot more. . . . With him, it's more [the loss of] a parent, with her, it's [the loss of] a friend. . . . She was someone I could just call and talk to and she'd go, "Oh, that's wonderful." And she would show off things that I did. . . . I don't have that in anyone else I know. You can feel supported, but not like Mom. Mom would show my picture to everyone. It was in the newspaper a couple of times and she would take it to the beauty parlor and show everybody.

The life course paths of parents and children overlap and evolve over time. Children age and begin to appreciate the older generation; parents also change, sometimes developing a greater appreciation for the child. A thirty-eight-year-old woman said of her father, "The older he got, I think he started realizing he couldn't make all of his four children's lives perfect, so he kind of gave up a little bit. . . . He seemed to turn into a happier person." Likewise, a thirty-one-year-old man described his father: "We never tended to be close. It wasn't until later that my dad came around in his emotional composition."

Lost Opportunities

Not all parents represent positive qualities that are missed by their children. As we saw in the last chapter, lives impacted by neglectful, abusive, or impaired parents can endure long after the parents die. Adults who associate a parent with negative traits and memories often must come to terms with their lifelong experience of criticism and perhaps an absence of love after the parent dies. In some instances, these adults say that they lost nothing or that their parent's death means the loss of bad parts of their life.

I took a close look at adults who grew up with critical, unloving, and dysfunctional parents. For these individuals, parent loss can symbolize both the loss of an opportunity to have a "good" parent and the missed opportunity to experience a positive, reciprocal relationship with the parent. In the next chapter, we see that these losses can motivate adults to change in dramatic ways that are directly linked to resolving old issues with the parent.

Parent As Critic

Some adults remember their parent as a relentless critic who always made the child feel like a failure. Like Bridget, forty-seven, many individuals who described the difficulties of a critical parent expressed some relief following the death:

> It's a sad commentary on our relationship, but any feeling of loss is outweighed by a feeling of freedom from constant scrutiny. It would have been much more difficult to deal with his death had we been very close emotionally.... Recently, when discussing my father's death with a friend, she asked me if I missed him and my response was, "I miss what might have been more than I miss what was."

Although an adult may feel a sense of liberation following the death of a difficult or critical parent, this relief does not preclude the possibility that the child also has some positive symbolic images of the parent. The poet Anne Sexton was tortured by thoughts of her neglectful and competitive mother, yet she nonetheless strongly identified with and admired her. Before her mother's death, Sexton said, "Part of me would be free if she died. It would also be awful – I would dissolve."[6]

I saw a similar ambivalence in many of my interviews. Hannah, for example, who described her father as the "Rock of Gibraltar," was extremely proud and appreciative of his unwavering stability in raising his family, especially in light of her mother's mental illness. Yet Hannah also associated her father with oppression and criticism, and the loss of his condemnation has freed her:

> He had a tendency to meddle and, in fact, he meddled a lot.... He really injected his opinions and he was judge and jury on a lot of things. He was, I guess, a little self-righteous. I hate to be critical ... [but] the truth of the matter is that he was very difficult to deal with when he did

not approve of things I did. . . . Sometimes he put a lot of
pressure on me and I think he judged me harshly on a lot of
things. . . . It is easier to be truer to myself now that I don't
have to deal with his approval or disapproval. . . . Now I
am unencumbered. . . . I can really do what I want and not
have to deal with that stamp of disapproval.

In particular, Hannah's father always disapproved of Hannah's
relationship with her husband of twelve years because the couple
did not plan to have children. Hannah's life has changed in many
ways since her father's death. Although she has lost a steady presence in her life, she feels freer to enjoy the relationship with her
husband. She also finds more security and stability in her marriage
than she did before her critical father died. All in all, Hannah feels
better about herself now that her father is not here to disapprove
of her.

Fifty-year-old Mary is divorced and she too feels liberated from
a critical parent. Mary is the third of five children, and feels that
her parents saw her as the failure of the family:

I always felt like I was a disappointment to my parents. I'm
the one that failed in life. . . . My siblings all have college
degrees. They all have successful jobs. . . . They all have
successful marriages. All their kids are great.

Mary's parents took care of her after she divorced, along with
Mary's three-year-old child and three-week-old infant. Yet her
mother always let Mary know that she had failed, even after Mary's
elderly parents moved in with her:

I'd try to cook and she would gag and she told me I was
starving her to death. . . . Well I just didn't know what to

do. I really wanted to do right, but she didn't like any of the food. . . . She always made me feel like I was the most hateful person in the world. She was a generous, giving person, but in giving, she was also manipulative and controlling and she could make me feel guilty . . . and I always felt like I didn't have the right to be angry.

Mary was the dependable daughter – the one who took her parents in when they needed care – yet her mother continued to be critical:

Like one Christmas . . . I'd gained weight . . . and Mother made gifts for everyone. She sewed beautifully and made these poinsettia pillows for everyone but me. . . . She gave me a scale. I opened it and saw what it was and I just shoved it under the couch because it embarrassed me too much.

Now that her mother is dead, Mary is free – free to be angry and to be herself:

I feel angry at her and I shouldn't any more. . . . I miss her, but in a way her dying has also made me feel free; that I don't have to be criticized. . . . At first I worried about me, wondering how I'd do by myself, but I think that's the best thing that's happened to me.

Mary has changed a great deal since her mother's death. She is pursuing new interests and enjoying spending time alone, and she is newly focused on herself without feeling guilty about being self-centered.

As I emphasized earlier, a sense of liberation does not preclude a strong sense of loss. Some adults simply view their new freedom as a positive consequence of an otherwise painful experience. Even Mary feels a strong sense of loss at the same time that she feels freed to pursue her own interests and happiness:

> The hardest thing about losing your parents is they're the only people that are ever going to care about you so much. . . . Nobody will ever care as much for you as your parents.

Absence of Love

In Joyce Carol Oates's novel *We Were the Mulvaneys*, the father is unable to face his teenaged daughter, Marianne, after she is raped. He copes by sending his daughter away and breaking off all contact with her. Marianne's entire life is shaped by her father's apparent withdrawal of love. Years later, as her father lay dying, Marianne comes to him, yearning for recognition. She then pleads with her brother to confirm her father's love for her: "Marianne said wonderingly, 'Daddy did recognize me, I think . . . I guess he's forgiven me? I mean – he loves me again, he's not ashamed of me?' "[7]

Just as some parents represent unconditional love for their children, others symbolize the absence of love. This theme is often linked to lost opportunities in that the adult child realizes that there will be no future chance to obtain love from the parent.

Diane is an accomplished and admired teacher. Although she has been happily married for twenty-seven years, she still cries over memories of a childhood devoid of parental love. Diane and her four sisters idolized their father when they were children. But

Diane's parents were alcoholics and had a violent relationship. Although they were affectionate with one another, they were never affectionate toward their daughters, and the girls never felt love or admiration from them:

> My parents never expressed love to their children.... They would not give emotionally...we were just asking for something they didn't have....None of us girls ever did anything wrong. We never got into trouble. We were in fifty million activities....No one paid attention to us. We just did it.

Diane and her sisters took care of one another throughout life. They loved one another and talked about their frustration with their parents. Shortly after Diane's father died, she and her sister Adele had a heart-to-heart talk:

> Adele said, "I know I have told you before but I want you to know that you are special." My parents never did that. They never just sat down and said, "There is no one that could take your place." This was something I couldn't imagine my parents doing. They would never give.

Almost all of the adults I talked with who felt unloved by their parents continue to feel hurt and helpless by this absence of love even after the parent's death. It is difficult for most adults to fill this emotional void even if they find love in marriage, friends, and their own children. There is a sense that at one's core, some deficiency must reside. Diane echoes this emptiness:

> If your parents don't love you, who could possibly love you?...Was something unlovable about us? We're good

people. . . . Maybe they didn't know how. . . . We all wanted their love.

Adults for whom a parent or parents continue to represent an absence of love often have a difficult time recovering from their loss. These adults have always hoped that love would eventually be forthcoming from the parent, and the parent's death terminates this hope.

Dysfunctional Parent

Dysfunctional parents may have social and personal problems that make their behavior and their presence in their children's lives unpredictable. Such parents may be alcoholic, violent, mentally ill, involved in volatile marital relationships, incompetent, or involved in their child's life to an unhealthy degree. As we saw in the last chapter, having a dysfunctional parent often permeates an individual's entire life story.

Diane, who felt the extreme absence of love in her childhood, grew up with two alcoholic parents. Her father also suffered from manic depression and her parents were physically violent with one another. Her father's many problems made childhood difficult:

> He was always drinking. . . . He would come in and would have had too much to drink. . . . My parents would have words. My mother was very low-key quiet, but then she had this temper. . . . She would just lose it and there would be dishes thrown and screaming. Then the next day, nothing would be said. . . . One time a friend spent the night. . . . We came in from the movie and there were dishes broken

in the kitchen. I turned to my friend and said, "Oh, no big deal." . . . But I was mortified.

Diane's father was also violent with Adele, Diane's favorite sister:

> She would take it to the limit. . . . They would physically go at each other. It was frightening to me because it seemed really out of control and he would slap her and she would slap back and then he would nearly kill her. . . . I wanted it to be quiet. I just wanted them in their corners, no chaos. . . . If he said something was black and I knew it was pink, I would say, "Black it is."

Diane says that she did not want a different father. She simply wanted her own father to be stable and loving, and on some level, she always believed that he might become the father she wished for. The pain of her loss is, in large part, the pain of knowing that her need will never be satisfied.

The Lost Opportunity to Have a "Good" Parent

The child within the adult never loses the need to be loved by the parent, but finally, through death, the child loses the possibility for love. When I met with the bereaved, they often spoke of missed opportunities for developing a different kind of relationship with their parent or for resolving difficulties with their parent prior to his or her death.

Lorrie struggles with the troubled relationship that she had with her father, who died three years ago, and she continues to yearn for a better relationship than the one they shared. Lorrie's father did not live with Lorrie and her mother for most of Lorrie's childhood. He had a serious alcohol problem and was abusive toward Lorrie's mother when he visited. After Lorrie graduated from high school, she decided to make a strong effort to have a more involved relationship with her father, but unless he was drinking heavily, he ignored her. When he was drinking, he allowed her to spend time with him, but he was abusive:

> He would get drunk or have a few beers and he would talk to me more like a man would talk to a son than the way a man would talk to a daughter. . . . It bothered me a lot. . . . He was a hard ass. The only time I could really have a conversation with him was when he had had a few beers. . . . Oh, he'd get mad. He had a temper. . . . He and I would fight. . . . And, then, like in a week, something would happen and I'd feel so close to him again. . . . When he was drinking, he was emotional. . . . He'd call and it'd be like, "Shit, he's loaded, here we go." And my husband would know I'm going to be on the phone an hour. But that was okay. Because I liked it when he called me. I loved it when he called and just wanted to talk to me.

Lorrie so wanted a relationship – any relationship – with her father that she appreciated even his late-night, abusive, drunken calls. I asked Lorrie what she felt she lost when he died:

> I felt that there could have been more of a relationship there. I can't believe that I miss him as much as I do. All the conflict, all the fighting, all the nasty things . . . there were a lot of years missed, a lot of a relationship missed.

Similarly, Amber, forty-eight, is coping with the loss of a mother who never treated her very well:

> My mother was not an emotionally well-stuck together lady. . . . She was very narcissistic, very controlling, very insecure. Most of my life we had a role reversal. Nothing like at the very end, but she was very sickly and [she] controlled [the family] with her symptoms. . . . Particularly me. . . . It was a love/hate relationship. . . . I loved my mother dearly, always did, always will. I did not like the woman. She was not a likeable person. She was mean as a snake and borderline evil . . . very volatile. . . . She was emotionally, verbally abusive.

Amber's mother died of complications from Alzheimer's disease. Her mother's mental condition deteriorated significantly in her last years. Two years before her death, she was unable to care for herself and her doctors recommended that she enter a nursing home. Amber would not consider this option and she took her mother into her home, providing the bulk of hands-on care that her mother required. Surprisingly, after an unhappy childhood in which Amber cared for her difficult mother, caring for her sick and elderly mother was an easy task to bear:

> It was like taking care of a little baby. I wanted to nurture her because she seemed so tiny and fragile. And, for the first time in my life. . . . I did not dislike her. There was no way to be angry at or hate someone that had reached that point in life.

Amber may have found it easier to care for her mother, in part, because, for the first time in Amber's memory, her mother was not critical and abusive. What did Amber lose with her mother's death?

> The chance to keep trying to make her whole emotionally.... I held out hope that I could get through to her and make her a happy person.... There was this fantasy hope in there somewhere that I could somehow make her contented and comfortable with herself.... I've lost that chance.... So I have to look at it as "we did the best we could." But it's sad. I grieve, I think, for what I never had more than the fact that my mother died.... There's something in there that's still unresolved.... I wanted desperately to earn her approval and I wonder sometimes if the grieving isn't more for what I wanted her to be and give to me all my life that she never could.... That thing I could never feel, I could never get from her, which was the unconditional-type parental love, the nurturing.

Adults like Lorrie and Amber describe the never-to-be-fulfilled desire to have a well-adjusted and loving parent. These adults typically spend most of their lives hoping to have something more from a mother or father. As long as the parent remained alive, the child could continue to hope, perhaps even deliberately work to create a more desirable relationship with the parent. The death of the parent means the death of this hope and a stopping point for reflection and reassessment of self.

Missed Opportunity to Give Back to the Parent

Just as some adult children struggle with the loss of a chance to have a "good" parent, others feel that the opportunity to be a good or dutiful child has passed them by. Some adults express a desire to reciprocate the love and duty that the parent had long provided.

David's mother committed suicide two months before our interview and he is trying to come to terms with why his mother ended her life. The death was unexpected and David had never considered her to be depressed or emotionally disturbed. In retrospect, he realizes that his mother was under a great deal of stress: She was going through a divorce, working long hours, and experiencing financial difficulty. Throughout our interview, David repeatedly emphasized his strong regret over having not done more for his mother. When asked what he lost with her death, David said:

> There are a lot of things I wanted to do for her 'cause she did a lot of things for us when we were growing up. Looking back now, there's a lot of things that I could have done for her. I feel like I wanted to get to know her better. . . . I have some things in my desk at work that I was going to send her. I just kept putting it off. . . . Just little things that I wanted to do that I didn't get to do. I was going to send her some flowers . . . but I don't have her address at work. . . . I had some pictures of my little boy and he drew some pictures for Grandma . . . but I just kept putting it off and I wish I would have got that to her. I don't know if it would have made a difference . . . but I would have liked to let her know that I was thinking about her.

Greg's father died almost three years ago, when Greg was thirty-five years old. Greg always felt close to his father, but he now mourns the lost opportunity to have a more reciprocal relationship with him:

> I lost the opportunity to know him as a man. He was always an adult, grown-up, authority figure. I would like to have talked to him as equals, to share *his* dreams, successes, failures. I wish I could have heard more about his boyhood, his army days in World War II, his days between the army and his marriage. I would like to have given him the opportunity to not be the father now and then.

For some adults, such lost opportunities lead to feelings of guilt, not around the parent's illness or death, but about long-term issues in past interactions with him or her. Other adults express guilt over not having been more appreciative and involved with their parent. Bill is one of six children from a poor and hard-working family. He left home when he was quite young, and although he stayed in touch by phone during the last few years, he seldom visited. Now Bill feels that his mother sacrificed a lot for him and his siblings, and he feels guilty for not giving more of himself to her: "I regret not being a better son. She would call and say, 'Billy, you need to take better care of this and that.' . . . I regret not being a better listener."

CONCLUSION

In my work with the bereaved, I find that most adults carry with them very specific symbolic images of their parents. When asked about these images, adults quickly and readily respond with little need to evaluate or formulate their views. Symbolic meanings emerge through a series of interactions with another person; in the case of parents, symbolic meanings arise through a lifetime of interactions. Because these interactions affect the way in which adults come to view themselves, the symbolism of the parent-child relationship can lead to either psychological distress or feelings of recovery following the parent's death. Some clinicians argue that the bereaved have more trouble recovering from the loss of closer and more dependent relationships, while others argue that it is more difficult to recover from the loss of ambivalent or conflicted relationships.[8] I find that a moderate view of parents as loving, but not as the most important source of love in one's life, seems to best facilitate recovery following the loss. Children who believe that their parents represent positive values such as stability and a sense of connection among generations also may have more wherewithal to cope with their parent's death because they are able to carry these gifts forward as they grow into adulthood. For those who do not have such positive associations, painful images of the past can linger to influence the shape of their future identity.

4

TURNING POINT IN
ADULTHOOD

I'm a different person and I will continue to be a different person. People have to realize that most of us will lose our parents in our lifetimes; even though it's a common experience, it does not diminish its impact. TINA. AGE THIRTY-FIVE

I've changed a lot since she died. By going to school and making myself try real hard. By staying sober when it's the hardest thing for me to do. By losing weight. I've lost twenty-five pounds so far....I've matured more. I don't worry as much about what people think of me. SUSAN. AGE THIRTY-TWO

Major life events can trigger turning points in adult life. Such catalysts can provide us with opportunities to recast self-conceptions, values, and beliefs. Some of the most common predictable life events of adulthood include marriage, the birth of a child, and widowhood.[1] Over the last hundred years, the timing and occurrence of these major events of adulthood have become much less predictable. During the same period, however, the death of a parent has become much more predictable as an event of middle adulthood. In fact, today the death of a parent is the most predictable major life event of people aged thirty-five to sixty.

The occurrence of a major life event can evoke dramatic self-reassessment and change. Stress researcher Jill Kiecolt argues that this reassessment occurs because it may help the individual to cope with the life transition and to reduce any resulting stress and emotional upset.[2] For example, following a divorce, a woman may become much more career-focused in an attempt to connect with others and stay busy in order to avoid troubling thoughts.

The way we respond to any major life transition is shaped, in part, by the symbolic meaning that the transition represents. For example, what does it mean to be a divorced person rather than a married person? The answers to the questions "Who am I?" and "How will I operate in the world?" can change dramatically following significant life transitions. Personal reassessment occurs partly because the individual seeks ways of fitting into a world where the demands and opportunities have changed. In this sense, the social context takes on new meaning. Psychologists Nancy Cantor and Sabrina Zirkel argue that "even familiar tasks such as 'finding intimacy' or 'being independent' really come to mean something entirely different in a new life period or setting."[3]

A parent's death is also highly symbolic in that it portends the bereaved adult's own mortality in a way that no other death can. A parent's death propels the social and psychological transition from childhood to adulthood. We suddenly recognize that there is no longer a parent to turn to; that there is no longer a choice about whether or not to be self-reliant. Even adults who did not rely greatly on their parent may experience the feeling of being on their own for the first time.

Developmental psychologists refer to the period between the ages of thirty-five and sixty-four as midlife, a time when adults tend to become less self-centered and more focused on relationships with others. Life course scholars Ravenna Helson and Abigail

Stewart argue that midlife is often a period of transition, that the "middle-aged are close to the height of their powers, yet also aware of an approaching decline. They are the bridge between the generations . . . concerned with reevaluating their lives."[4] Because the death of a parent occurs against this developmental backdrop of increasing midlife concern with relationships and generational linkages, it can be a catalyst for change.

DIRECTING CHANGE IN THE SELF

After his or her parent dies, an adult may be particularly motivated to change the self in order to revive, revere, escape, or reject the parent. The particular motivation for personal change depends on the adult's life history, particularly on his or her past experiences with the parent.

Reviving the Parent

Adults for whom parents evoke positive feelings and memories often change in ways that make them more like the parent who died. These adults are likely to adopt new roles, behaviors, and attitudes that emulate those of the parent. Such emulation is a primary feature of early childhood. In later childhood, adolescence, and early adulthood, the child may rebel against some of the parent's qualities, but this rebellion seems to diminish with age. The desire to emulate the parent appears to accelerate to a new high after a parent dies. In part, this is an attempt to keep the parent present.

Children initially develop a sense of self in relation to the parent, in large part by identifying with the parent and internalizing the parent's wishes and values. Psychologists Hazel Markus and

Susan Cross argue that, through the process of internalization, the child:

> ... takes on the attitudes, beliefs, and behaviors of another and makes them one's own. . . . [W]hen individuals have strong emotional ties to others, they will emulate these others in the hope of maintaining these ties and gaining love and acceptance. . . . [I]dentification with a parent, for example, should lead to internalization of the parent's attitudes, beliefs, and characteristic behaviors.[5]

The parent plays such a powerful role in shaping the child's sense of self that the parent can be said to reside within the child throughout life. Identification with the parent in early childhood is considered a normal phase of development. Likewise, grief expert Therese Rando argues that identification with a deceased loved one, if not extreme to the point of obscuring recognition of the death, is a normal part of bereavement:

> Identification with the deceased occurs first as a way of perpetuating the mental image of the loved one to avoid feeling the pain of loss. By temporarily preserving the loved one, identification allows the mourner to work at the process of withdrawing and modifying emotional ties without being overwhelmed. Later, it helps to conserve the lost object while adding to the ego, thereby contributing to the enrichment of the personality.[6]

Identification with the deceased person may follow the death of any significant other. However, the process of identification following a parent's death is unique because the parent is already an internalized figure dating back to the origin of the child's sense of self. The process of identification following the parent's death results in an updating of and adding to what has always been within the self: How any particular individual changes reflects the dynamics of the lifelong relationship with the parent. The adult self is altered in a way that further internalizes the parent *and* reflects the new absence of the external parent. A new phase of adulthood is entered in which the adult is no longer a child to a parent; rather, the adult self is updated so that the adult becomes his or her own parent. The child may change in ways that make him or her more similar to the parent who died. By incorporating the parent into the self, the adult revives the parent and keeps the parent present.

Most bereaved adults I have talked with have a sense of losing an important part of themselves after a parent dies. Some change in the self represents an attempt to hold on to that part of themselves. Although the child's own identity has always reflected the parent's influence and, in this sense, the parent has lived within the child all along, many adults begin to feel more aware of their parent's influence after the parent dies. Many adults say that they see the parent in themselves more after the parent died than they did prior to the loss. After her father died, fifty-two-year-old Helen told me, "Who I am is him, but I didn't realize that ... until he died. . . . I realized my father lives on through me in a way."

Adults may see the parent in themselves more, in part, because the aspects of the self that reflect the parent are magnified after the parent dies and as postbereavement identification with the parent takes hold.

I asked Helen what she started seeing in herself that was so like her father. She explained:

I realized the things I love and value are the things he loved and valued and I learned that from him. . . . What I'm saying is that these things were absorbed. . . . Before he died his influence wasn't evident to me. Realizing his influence was just astounding. . . . It's the most beautiful experience. I just wish . . . I could talk to him about this. . . . If only I could tell him.

Seeing her father within herself is comforting to Helen. By identifying with her father and beginning to recognize his influence on her, Helen revives her father; she keeps him alive by letting him live within herself. As a result, her definition of self is evolving.

After a parent dies, many adults begin to consider their parent's views and advice more than they did prior to the loss. They are more likely, when making decisions, to consider what the parent would have done in similar circumstances, and they are more likely to consider their parent's advice when making decisions. Several years after their deaths, Kim continues to visit the cemetery where her parents are buried:

It's a very serene place, kind of out in the country. . . . I spend every Sunday afternoon for about an hour just sitting out in the cemetery and that would give me time to unload all the stress from the week. Just to say, "Okay, Mom, Dad, here's what's going on. Help me work through this. What am I going to do here? What am I going to do there?" And although they do not talk back to you, they do mentally because you're raised by them. So that you pick up their thought processes an awful lot and you pick up their ideas and they kind of, in that way, help you solve problems.

By identifying with the parent, the adult gains an additional vantage point from which to make decisions about life. In this sense, the self gains new dimensions and ways of viewing and coping with life.

Of course, not all parents are admired or admirable. Identifying with the parent can occur even when the parent's traits are viewed negatively. When the parent's negative qualities are central to the memory of the parent, the child sometimes feels compelled to replicate them. This is especially true when the child feels that he or she failed to please the parent in life.

Dan, twenty-five, was the youngest of seven children and had a very intense, conflict-ridden relationship with his father. Now he continues to feel that he cannot please his father, even though his father is dead. Note how Dan talks about his father, using the present tense:

> I'm afraid of him being disappointed in me or not being proud of me. . . . It's basically because of him that he has such a strong impact on my life. I can't bear to disappoint him, to shame him.

Dan describes his father as an impatient, angry, and critical man, yet Dan defends his father by emphasizing that he understands how having so many children, some of them quite rebellious, could bring out the worst in a father. Dan is expending enormous energy to avoid negative memories of his father: "I try not to think about him because I don't want to get myself down. I don't want to let my guard down."

Now that Dan's father is dead, Dan is becoming more and more like his father in a seeming attempt to obtain posthumous approval. He is even taking his father's place as a caretaker for his mother:

> I feel that I am my father's son. . . . He is in me. . . . That's where I feel his presence. . . . My mom even says I remind

her so much of Dad. . . . I am the epitome of my father. . . . Everything that my father used to do I find in me. Like coming home at five o'clock and finding somebody in my chair. . . . I am angry. . . . I am lacking patience. He really lacked patience.

Dan is becoming like his father, even though he recognizes that his father was a difficult man and even though he does not want the responsibility of taking his father's place. He is compelled to do so because he still craves his father's approval.

For instance, Dan is not fully comfortable with his role as caretaker but feels compelled to honor his father by assuming that role:

My mom used to call my father her sanity. . . . Now I have to constantly be there for my mother. . . . I feel I can't move out. I can't do anything. I have to think about her first. . . . I don't want it. I've got to accept it. . . . One reason is to honor my father. . . . I want to be able to feel like I'm free, which I don't feel like I am. . . . I won't abandon her. That's all there is to it. . . . I am my father's son. I honor my father. . . . I want to be the type of man I know he would want me to be. Yes, that's it.

If identification with the deceased parent is extreme and the parent exhibited dysfunctional traits, the parent's life may become a self-fulfilling prophecy for the bereaved adult. Some individuals seem to follow an almost deterministic course in life by living the same life as their parent; in some cases, like Dan's, this happens even when the adult says that he or she does not want it to happen. Susan, thirty-two, is replicating her mother's life choices even though those choices undermined her mother's happiness. Susan's father sexually abused her and her sisters, yet her mother remained married to him until he died. He was a difficult man and Susan despised him.

Since her mother died, Susan has begun to assume many of her mother's roles, especially in taking care of her sisters, one of whom is an alcoholic. Susan also strongly identifies with her mother in a way that influences how she deals with her own abusive and alcoholic husband. Because Susan strongly identifies with her mother and because her mother did not leave an abusive husband, Susan now feels that her marriage will follow the same course as her mother's:

> I think about her every day and I dream about her every night. Everything I go through I think, "Mama had to go through this too – having three kids and going to school." When my husband and I are fighting, I think of her failed relationship and think, "Well, she went through this too." It helps because it makes me feel like she is there, that I am not alone.

Susan accepts that her own unhappy relationship will not improve and cannot be altered; her memory of her mother actually leads her to accept this situation more than she did prior to the loss. Living her mother's life comforts Susan because it means keeping her mother by her side. Susan's need to stay by her mother now undermines her own happiness, yet she does not seem to recognize this connection.

In the end, the self may be modified to be more like the parent. This is a comfort to most adults, a way to hold on to the loved and admired parent. But for some individuals, like Dan and Susan, it may mean the addition or amplification of negative dimensions of the self. In the short run, some comfort may be derived from keeping the parent present and trying to resolve old issues with him or her. In the long run, personal and interpersonal problems may result. Most bereaved adults are not fully aware that they are reliving the parent's life, yet even when they are aware, it seems to be very difficult to steer themselves along another path.

Revering the Parent

To revere the parent is to change in ways that honor him or her, by becoming a person the parent would admire and be proud of. Like those who are motivated by a desire to revive the parent, those who are motivated to revere the parent often change in order to become more like him or her. However, revering the parent differs in that the main motivation of the child is to pay homage to the parent. One of the forces behind revering the parent is an increased appreciation of him or her. Many of the bereaved adults that I have spoken with tell me that they began to appreciate their parent more after the parent died.

Karen, now forty-four, grew closer to her mother after her father died. Until that time, Karen's mother had always been very critical of Karen. Now that both of her parents are gone, Karen focuses on the positive features of the relationship with both of her parents:

I appreciate both my mother and father more now and all they did for me. I think once your parents die, you tend to forget about the negative things and you remember the positive things about them, about your relationship with them, about how they treated you and brought you up.

This greater appreciation for the parent, along with an increased tendency to see the parent in oneself, bodes well for self-image and sense of worth.

Some bereaved adults who strongly admired their parent make a conscious effort to emulate the parent. Bill, forty-four, is from a large and loving family and has four siblings. His mother, who died at the age of sixty-two, "made sure all of us stuck together." Bill describes her as "a brilliant lady" and a loving mother. He is very proud of how she, although poor, worked hard to help him get through college. Bill finished college and became a teacher. Yet Bill did not visit his mother as much as he feels he should have, and he continues to feel guilty about an early first marriage, at the age of twenty, to a pregnant girlfriend – a marriage that ended in divorce. Now that his mother is gone, Bill desperately wants to honor her memory. He does so, in part, by changing himself to become more like the mother he admired and more like the kind of person he knows his mother would want him to be:

> I want to be able to do more for people, like Mama did. . . .
> I really want to be the type of father my father was to
> me. . . . I'm trying to live a more Christian life. . . . I guess
> that's why I said I pray to Mama. . . . "Please help me to do
> these things that I know you would want me to do: Being
> a good father, a Christian person, in my occupation as a
> teacher, and being caring and sincere."

On some level, Bill recognizes that he is trying to communicate with his mother, to convince her that he is what she wanted him to be. He conveys this by providing advice to others going through parental loss:

> After the fact, it doesn't help to talk to your mother, so it's better to go ahead and say, "Hey Mom, I love you." Now, when she can respond back to you – instead of saying it when they are deceased. . . . It may be hard for you to say when they are alive, but it's better to say it when they can really hear you instead of saying it to a spirit.

While some adults feel fated to reliving their parent's mistakes, other adults revere their parent by avoiding the parent's mistakes. For instance, Tom was very close to his father and he strongly identified with him, especially in adulthood. Father and son were physicians who practiced medicine together for ten years. Tom says, "I always wanted to be just like him." After his father died, Tom began to realize how much his own miserable marriage resembled that of his parents. He strongly empathized with his father, who was quite unhappy in marriage. In turn, Tom made a decision to leave his wife in order to avoid his father's fate:

> My mother and father stayed together and stayed married even though their relationship was not a good one. . . . I'm like him in so many ways that I just said to myself that I don't think he made the right decision to stay married to my mother for as long as he did and I wish that he had done something about it earlier. . . . He's told me many times that he made a mistake in not getting a divorce, but that once he passed a certain age there was really no point in doing it. . . . I'm forty-four and there's a sense of running out of time that is made more apparent by the death of a

parent, even though he was eighty. It seemed to me that he deserved a better fate than that and my choice was to not follow that same road that he had followed and wind up like him . . . so I decided to take a different path. . . . I thought it would be . . . a healthy thing to separate for a while. It's helped me deal with my grief in the loss of my father.

By rescuing himself from an unhappy marriage, Tom is rescuing a piece of his father as well. In a sense, by separating from his wife, Tom is honoring the memory of his father. Of course, Tom's own personal changes and choices have profound effects on his relationship with his wife and children.

Escaping the Parent

Some adults change in ways that were unthinkable prior to a parent's death because of the parent's judgmental nature. In other cases, these changes were avoided in the past simply because they would have hurt the parent. Many adults provide moving descriptions of how the death liberated them from their old life and their old self.

Tom, the man who left his wife in order to avoid his father's fate of living in an unhappy marriage, had another reason for leaving his wife, a reason motivated by his mother's death. Tom's mother died six months before his father died. Tom was never close to his mother and he felt like a happier person after her death:

She lavished attention on all of the children to a fault. To a serious fault. . . . She felt that all the children owed her something. . . . She was domineering. She dominated my father. She dominated everyone she came into contact with.... She could be extraordinarily tough and she was difficult to love as an adult. In fact, she was alienated from all three of her children after they reached puberty.... She exerted such influence over all of us that she kept us all in turmoil.... My mother tried to play us off against each other.... After she died everybody seemed to be happier in many respects. I don't say that facetiously. My father, I think, enjoyed the last six or eight months of his life.

Tom felt liberated by his mother's death:

I felt freedom from worrying about being criticized.... Fear of parental disapproval was, I'm sure, a contributing factor to keeping my wife and me together.... Her death has encouraged me to try and enjoy life more.... I guess when you relax and think of it in those terms, it might make me a more effective doctor.... It's related to the feeling that perhaps time is running out and so the question is, "if not now, when?"

I asked Tom how he thinks each of his parents would view the separation from his wife:

Well, I think my father would've approved.... He probably would've tried to talk me out of moving out and separating because I have three children. But having done it.... I don't think he would disapprove of what I've done. And, now, there's just no doubt about it, my mother would definitely disapprove and would summon up all the, you

know, all the resources at hand to try to control my behavior to a more acceptable standard.

A new sense of freedom often leads to behavioral change and
important life choices. Some adults decide to take a chance and
change religions or jobs. Others move to new geographic locations.
Some, like Tom, describe how the death of a parent frees them to
leave an unhappy marriage, to no longer worry about the parent's
reaction to divorce.

Rejecting the Parent

Most adults dislike some of their parent's characteristics or behaviors. Those dislikes can be quite strong. As long as the parent is
alive, the child, out of fear or respect, may not openly oppose the
parent on those fronts. After the parent dies, however, these negative characteristics can come into sharp focus, especially if they
were issues for the child throughout life. Some individuals change
themselves in ways that directly oppose negative characteristics
of the parent in order to ensure that he or she will not be like the
parent. Desley, for example, actively works to avoid being like her
mother:

> A lot of things I've done for the past five or six years have
> been in total opposition to my mother's life. She was a
> woman who, twenty years ago, decided that life . . . was
> over for her. She sat down and waited twenty years to die.
> I started back to work about five years ago and I'm going
> back to school – both are a result of my desire not to be
> like her. . . . The death of a mother, in a way, frees you.

Since her mother's death, Desley feels energized to pursue relationships, work, and leisure activities that defy her mother's passive, withdrawn approach to life:

> I think that a lot of women are afraid of surpassing their mothers or being better or having more, and I think that while she was alive, I was more aware of that. And now because she's not here to know what's going on ... it's easier for me.

THE SELF IN TIME

The death of a parent marks a rite of passage as we make the final step into adulthood – as we lose our status as child to a parent. Stepping ever closer to death, we also develop a keener sense of personal mortality after a parent dies.

Transition to Adulthood

Many sons and daughters describe a sense of sudden adulthood as a significant consequence of their parent's death, and this realization is almost always viewed in a positive light.

Karen lost both of her parents over a period of eight days. She feels that she had little choice in making the final passage to adulthood. Karen was never particularly dependent on her parents. When Karen's sister was nine and Karen was fifteen, their mother developed a serious alcohol problem. Karen largely took over the domestic tasks and assumed the role of mother toward both her sister and her mother. Thus, Karen has acted as an adult for most of her life, even in relation to her parents. But after her parents died, being an adult took on new meaning:

> You are never prepared for the feeling of suddenly being alone – parentless – an orphan. No matter how old you are. It makes you feel like you *have* to grow up. You *have* to be an adult now. You *have* to rely on yourself because they aren't there anymore.

A key component of adult status is a stronger sense of being responsible for others as well as oneself. This change is manifested in different ways. The adult often takes over some of the deceased parent's roles in caring for other family members. Susan is a recovering alcoholic. After her mother died, she took over her mother's role of caring for her sisters:

> My younger sisters and me, we get along better now. . . . It just makes me feel better knowing Renae's there because she is part of Mama. My younger sister is spoiled rotten. . . . Now I try a lot harder to put up with things about her that I don't like. . . . I feel kind of motherly to Renae and Cathy now because Renae is drinking again and I know what that is like. . . . I feel I should help her; that I should take over some of Mama's place. Cathy . . . gets depressed a lot. . . . I feel I should help her too because she relied a lot on Mama.

Susan feels that her mother's death has evoked profound change in her life:

> It makes me feel like my whole life has changed. . . . I started school right after my mom died – to be a teacher.

She knew about that and was looking forward to it. She was going to be real proud of me because she knew that I had quit high school and gone into the Navy and started to drink. She was real proud that here I was at thirty . . . going back to school. . . . Becoming a teacher will make me feel better. I will have achieved something.

In addition to taking care of her sisters, Susan is now playing a greater role in parenting herself: "I'm now the oldest generation and I don't have anyone comforting me. . . . I've got to come up with the wisdom myself."

After the death of a parent, some individuals place a higher priority on their children and families, on mentoring the next generation, or on creative works. This focus results in a significant change in adult identity and sense of self. In part, this type of change is motivated by a growing inability to deny the eventual inevitability of mortality and the need to leave some kind of legacy behind. For example, Bobby, forty-one, is spending more time with his six-year-old son and talking to him about his grandfather. Bobby focuses more on passing things along from his own father to his son. Jeannie, thirty-one, doesn't have children, but her mother's death heightens Jeannie's commitment to starting a family.

Prior to a parent's death, most adults have had little contact with illness and loss. Recognizing a different dimension of normal everyday life – and the difficulties associated with it – many individuals describe how they are much more capable and willing to help others now that they have experienced their own loss. It leads to an increasing concern with contributing to humanity and community. The bereaved often feel that they have something important and unique to pass along to others. Christine, forty-two, explains: "A positive result of the death is a deepening of my sensitivity to the suffering of others; a further ability and ease of being with people who are dying or have had a friend or relative die." Carol, thirty-four, does more now to help others: "I now have the ability to understand what people go through in caring for someone who is very ill. . . . When someone is ill or has a loved one ill or someone has just lost a loved one, I have learned not to say, 'let me know if I can do anything.' Now I actually bring them meals, clean their house or help with household chores or errands without being asked."

The Mortal Self

A parent's death can force adults to think about their own mortality in a way they have not in the past. In her biography, Kathenne Graham talks about her own father's death in just this way: "[P]eople react in such complicated ways to any death, but particularly to the death of a parent, because a lot of what one feels is about oneself and the sense that nothing now stands between that self and dying."[7]

Recognition of one's own mortality can also alter one's outlook on life. Many bereaved individuals begin to see their own lives as short and fragile. Circumstances surrounding the parent's death may fuel this view. For instance, Michelle's father died unexpectedly of a heart attack at the age of fifty-eight and his premature death changed Michelle's philosophy on life:

He died so young. . . . I think anybody can die anytime. . . . I enjoy life more. I've slowed down a bit which I was beginning to do as I got older anyway. But I think it's accelerated – just to make sure I appreciate really little things.

That sounds very trite, but I really do it. . . . I feel really positive. I feel very alive and I'm appreciative for what's in my life. . . . You realize that there's nothing guaranteed. It really does change your whole way of looking at things.

Recognition of personal mortality may lead to very practical behaviors in terms of preparing for one's own death. These behaviors reflect real personal change in that individuals are beginning to recognize and come to terms with the finite quality of life. Kim, thirty-two, bought a burial plot so her family would not have to go through the stress of doing it for her. Mark, forty-seven, decided it was time to prepare a will.

Some parents prepare every detail of their funeral, burial, and estate settlement. This attention to detail is comforting to bereaved adult children, freeing them from making numerous, often difficult, decisions in the wake of the death. Other parents leave all the details to their children. Although some bereaved adults find the management of such details to be distracting and helpful, most find them to be stressful and upsetting. Either situation – having a well-prepared parent or having to cope with the strain of making decisions about funeral arrangements and estate settlements – can lead adults to make their own plans so that their children and loved ones will not have to deal with these matters in the future.

PERSONAL OUTLOOKS ON LIFE

The lens through which one views the world constitutes a dimension of the self. Individual outlooks on life may be primarily positive or negative in tone. Fortunately, following a parent's death, change in the direction of a more positive outlook on life is more common than change in a negative direction. Many bereaved adults say that they appreciate life more now than they did before their parent's death, and some of them view life as more meaningful. One of the clearest and most common changes in outlook is the recognition that life is short and should be lived more fully than in the past.

Yet a parent's death can trigger a shift toward darker world views. Some adults view life as more unfair and some feel more cynical than they did prior to the loss. A powerful predictor of a darkened world view is a difficult life history.

Difficult experiences with parents that are not resolved prior to death cause some individuals to feel bitter and more cynical about life. Of course, difficult childhood experiences can also cause individuals to be more bitter and cynical before the parent's death. Yet the death is a pivot point in that bitterness and cynicism may come to predominate even more heavily in the child. On the other hand, some adults feel liberated from a difficult childhood once the parent dies, and in these cases, their outlook on life may become more positive.

Darkened world views may also be tied to the suffering that a parent experienced prior to death. If the individual always felt that the world was a controllable and predictable place, yet his or her parent died suddenly or unexpectedly, he or she may re-define the world as a more unpredictable and dangerous place in order to make these world views compatible with personal life experiences.[8] Nina, age thirty, was extremely close to her father her entire life. He was a confidant and a buffer between Nina and her difficult mother. Nina describes her father as a gentle and law-abiding man. Almost one year before our interview, a stranger murdered her fifty-year-old father. At the time of the murder, Nina

was on her way to a family get-together. She describes how she
found out about her father's death:

> I was coming down Green Road, about to turn toward
> my sister's house. It was dark by then. They had the road
> blocked off so you had to turn on my sister's street. You
> couldn't see ahead. All you could see was the ambulance
> and flashing lights. I thought, "Oh God, there's been an
> accident." . . . Jill called and said, "Have you seen Dad?" . . .
> [I thought] maybe we should go check. . . . There were cops
> there. . . . This woman cop came up to me and she said, "I
> understand that you're trying to find out if that was a rela-
> tive of yours. What's his name?" And she said, "Well, I'm
> sorry to tell you, but he's dead." . . . A man had rear-ended
> my father. Then that man had gotten out and beaten him
> to death.

Since her father died, Nina has married and continues to work
full-time. Yet the unjust end to her father's life has profoundly
altered Nina's outlook on life:

> I used to be a fun person. I mean, a blast to have around.
> And you just don't have that in you any more. I don't
> know what other people tell you about grief, but it affects
> everything you do. I mean, I had a great sex life before. I
> don't think I'll ever have that back again. . . . It's just not
> a top priority anymore. It's just not important.

She also views life as more fragile and unpredictable than before:

> I worry about losing my husband all the time. . . .
> We're both much more careful people now. . . . I feel

more vulnerable. Something horrible can happen to me any day.

Negative world views may also be fueled by feelings of regret about the past relationship with the parent, regret over not making better use of last moments, not resolving old issues with the parent, and not managing the parent's health and medical care more effectively.

Many people feel tormented by medical decisions made or not made for a parent. This is almost always an unfair sentence for the adult. Most people lack the training and experience needed to make such medical decisions, even though they are often called upon to do so for a parent. Moreover, these decisions must be made during a stressful time, when the bereaved person is not at his or her strongest and clearest. Finally, it is impossible to know the final outcome of treatment or nontreatment in advance, yet adults feel pressured to strike a balance between requesting enough treatment for the possibility of cure and not inflicting unnecessary trauma on their parent.

Charles, fifty-four, tended to his mother's needs in later life. Sylvia was an independent, healthy, and active woman even into her eighties. She became sick only near the end of her life. Sylvia's kidneys were failing and she and her doctor decided that she should begin dialysis. Her doctor assured her that the dialysis would give her several more healthy years of life. Once Sylvia decided to try dialysis, Charles did what he could to encourage her about it:

But the pain of her dialysis treatment was so painful, was so horrible. . . . She said she had never experienced pain like that in her life. After the first treatment she went into a terrible decline. . . . I'm at the hospital, trying to keep upbeat and saying, "Boy, it will work – it's painful now, it's miserable, but after it's all done it will work." The next day I walked in her room and they are beating on her chest just like you would see on a soap opera. . . . I said, "No, she's been through enough." . . . The chaplain comes up and says her heart has started again. I said, "What does this mean, they started her heart again, what does this mean?" . . . There could be brain damage. . . . So I'm yelling in the room when they are banging on her chest. I'm saying, "She has a living will." I'm yelling, "The living will!" and they are saying, "No, the living will does not cover resuscitation."

Charles continues to question himself about what happened before Sylvia's death and wonders if he should have been more forceful in helping her make medical decisions and monitoring her health care:

When I think of her it's usually about how she died. It bothers me a lot that she was in pain and she knew that there were some desperate things happening. . . . She must have been terribly afraid. . . . There are certain things that happened in the two days at the hospital where she must have been frightened and in great pain. Those days strike me more than anything. I keep asking the question, was there another way it could have been handled? Was there another way to do it?

As we saw earlier, positive final days and hours before a parent dies can take on lasting meaning for the adult child. In some cases, when the parent made a yearned-for gesture toward the adult, the adult benefits. Similarly, difficult final moments can take on lasting and painful meaning for the adult child, casting a shadow on his or her usual way of looking at the world.

CONCLUSION

The death of a parent is a turning point in adulthood, a time of significant personal change. In fact, this may be the most important and active period of individual change that routinely occurs in adulthood.

The self is profoundly altered following a parent's death. Individuals change to become more or less like the parent who died. The direction of change is guided largely by the type of relationship the child had with the parent throughout life. Some become more similar to the parent in order to emulate and revere the parent. Any change that emulates the parent represents an attempt to hold on to the parent, to keep the parent within, and, in some instances, to resolve old issues with the parent. On the other hand, some individuals attempt to resolve old issues with the parent by changing to become less like him or her. In doing so, they act on their rejection of certain qualities of the parent. Many adults, especially those who had critical or judgmental parents, feel liberated by the death and feel freed to change in new directions never before dared: to divorce, for example, or simply to finally be true to oneself.

Clearly, the adult's life history, especially in relation to the parent, matters to the adult as much after the mother or father's death as it did before. The implications of the past relationship are tremendous and potentially momentous for personal change. This powerful relationship continues to shape the child's sense of self, even after the parent leaves the material world.

Fundamental change in the self is also triggered by the changing position of the self in time. After a parent dies, the child moves to the front line of mortality. The child becomes the next generation in line for death. This reality marks a rite of passage to adulthood as the adult loses the status of child to a parent and must become parent to the self. Adults gain a new sense of adult identity. They also develop a keener sense of the inevitability of personal mortality, making them appreciate life more, take better care of their health, and even to prepare for their own deaths.

5

INTIMATE RELATIONSHIPS

My husband has been a great source of strength to me throughout my mother's illness. He has been patient and has listened when others didn't want to listen anymore.

ANGIE, AGE TWENTY-NINE

My husband has a hard time with me and my emotional feelings about my mom. I feel like he wishes I'd get over it and go on. CORINNE, AGE THIRTY-NINE

The effects of parent loss on marital quality were striking and consistent in the national survey: More often than not, following a parent's death, marital quality deteriorates.[1] For example, among adults who did not experience a parent's death, conflict with their spouse changed very little over a three-year period. Moreover, the change that did occur tended to be in a positive direction. However, among those adults who lost a parent during this period, conflict with a spouse actually increased.

I was a bit surprised at the consistency of these negative effects across various aspects of couples' marriages. Certainly, it seemed plausible that the loss might bring couples closer together, providing an opportunity for a spouse to support and console the bereaved adult. So, for me, the results from the national survey raised as many questions as they answered. In my interviews with the bereaved, I found the answers to many of these questions.

Torn Asunder

Emotional needs run high after the death of a parent. Although most partners attempt to support the bereaved person, many desire more attention and support than they receive. In this context of need, several common problems seem to contribute to a decline in the quality of a marriage. There are gender differences in the need for support and the ability to meet those needs, and these differences can create hard feelings between a husband and wife. Some spouses are not empathic, either because they do not have the skills or because they did not like the parent who died. And, finally, the continuing distress in a bereaved person, along with high levels of need, can create strain in a relationship.

Failed Support

A spouse can make us feel loved, cared for, listened to, and understood. This emotional support, which is perhaps the most important ingredient of a good marriage, is especially important during difficult times because it helps adults to cope with and adjust to life crises. A recurrent theme in accounts of marital decline is that the bereaved began to feel disappointment and anger for not receiving the emotional support that was desired or needed. For example, Lois, thirty-seven, was very disappointed in her husband's inability to support her after her father died. It has been more than two years since the death and she continues to "hold a grudge" against her husband, Herb:

> My husband wasn't there for me during the whole pro-
> cess. He worked that much harder. He couldn't deal
> with it. . . . The day before my dad died, they put him on
> morphine. I knew he didn't have much longer. I called
> Herb. . . . The only way my husband could deal with it
> was – he went to work. . . . You know he couldn't deal with
> the dying part of it. It hurt me and I still hold a grudge
> because he wasn't there for me when I thought he needed
> to be, emotionally. . . . I just wanted him to be there. I told
> him, "Of all the times that I needed someone there, you
> couldn't be there for me." . . . Emotionally, I needed him
> more than I ever needed him before. . . . It's left a real sore
> spot and he can't understand why I can't get over it.

One problem for Lois stems from the kind of relationship she had with her parents and sisters throughout life. Lois was the "good girl" in the family, standing by her father and taking care of him even when the other sisters could not forgive him for his alcoholism and their difficult childhood. Now that her father is dead, Lois continues to have to take care of herself as well as her mother and everyone else. Although Lois has been a caregiver for many decades, she now wants Herb to relieve her of this role. Lois is "mad, irritated, annoyed, hurt." Their eighteen-year marriage will probably remain intact, but it has suffered a blow. Lois says, "I think we're probably pretty much just kind of coasting. . . . I hope I quit holding a grudge because he's a real good person. I just can't get over the fact that he couldn't have been there for me. I mean, I did it all myself."

Couples are, from their start, influenced by their life histories, and perhaps especially by the past with their parents. As we have already seen, adults undergo personal change after a parent dies, and the nature of that change is strongly linked to their unique life histories. For instance, Lois has been burdened since childhood with undue responsibility for others. Now that her parents are dead, she wants to be relieved of this sense of responsibility that was imposed on her as a child. She is ready for someone to finally take care of her. Herb, on the other hand, married a woman whose major role in life was being self-sufficient and caring for others. His father-in-law's death hasn't changed Herb's view of himself or his wife. The change in one partner and not the other can disrupt a couple's usual interactions and dynamics.

All of us face crises at different points in our lives. For those of us in relationships, each crisis affects not only us as individuals but our relationships as well. The death of a parent is a highly personalized life event for individuals, but as personal as it is, it has profound implications for relationships as the bereaved person needs and desires emotional support, understanding, and empathy from his or her partner. Although many adults indicate that their partner attempted to be helpful during the bereavement period, the help that was given often was not enough; this sets the stage for feelings of disappointment.

Part of the reason that bereaved individuals perceive a lack of sufficient support from their partner is that their need is so great. The person may have lost a parent figure who was a symbol of emotional support and nurturance. Even if the parent was not supportive of the child, this history of lack of support may only increase the felt need of the bereaved child to obtain support now. The spouse is a logical substitute for the parent. After all, classic marriage vows call for support of the spouse in sickness and in health; in good times and in bad. The spouse may be confused because the bereaved partner never needed so much support before; it is as if the rules have changed.

Bill could always rely on his mother to recognize his needs and respond to them. His wife, Dee, is not so forthcoming with her feelings and certainly not as solicitous of Bill in encouraging his expression of thoughts and feelings:

> Even talking on the telephone, Mama would say, "Billy, you got something on your mind, you need to go ahead and get it off your chest." . . . Mama knew how to push the right buttons just to get me to really talk to other people. . . . I guess you always expect your wife to be like your mother, so I was a little disheartened with my wife.

Bill wants his wife to be more like his mother in certain ways. But, overall, Bill's marriage has not really suffered much as a result of his mother's death because, in many respects, Dee already is a lot like his mother. Bill appreciates these qualities in his wife: "Dee is a wonderful mother, the way she takes care of our son. . . . She's like Mama. She's a very caring person."

In some cases, as we see below, the need to see the parent in the spouse undermines marital relationships. However, this has not occurred in Bill's marriage. First, Bill does see some of his mother's positive qualities in Dee. Second, the death of Bill's mother is a turning point in Bill's view of himself. Her death has highlighted the value of strong family ties and his mother's role in creating a loving and close family. As a result, Bill is more focused than ever before on nurturing the relationship with his wife as well as his son:

> Mama was, to me, a very holy person. She was very caring. . . . I don't see how she couldn't be in heaven. . . . She

and my grandmother and my older brother look down on me as an earthly person and just help me to be the Christian son, brother, and grandson that they really want me to be.

Gender, Emotions, and Support

Although Bill wanted his wife to be more nurturing, typically women are more likely than men to crave more emotional support from their partners. For instance, Lois knew how to ask for emotional support, but Herb did not know how to give her the support she wanted. This mismatch reflects a common gender dynamic in marriages. Both men and women need emotional support in times of crisis, but their ability to obtain and provide support diverges.[2] Women are more effective providers of emotional encouragement than are men, and men benefit from this conventional feminine skill. Women, such as Lois, are also more effective in asking for emotional support; however, their male partners, such as Herb, are often unable to provide it. Herb did, in fact, provide a certain kind of support. Lois felt exhausted and depleted after her father died. She lost weight and could not sleep. Herb sent her roses and encouraged her to quit her job. Although she did quit and she has thoroughly enjoyed the change in lifestyle, she wanted more from Herb. Lois describes Herb as "a real good-hearted person and he'd do anything for anybody but I don't think he knows how to show emotion or he doesn't want to show emotion."

Women often complain of their partner's inability or unwillingness to talk about the loss. They want their spouses to initiate the conversation. Cindy, thirty-nine, explains:

The subject of my father's death in the months following the death was never brought up unless I brought it up. His uncertainty and uneasiness of dealing with me and this situation made me very intolerant of him in general. I was almost angry with him because he was very passive about this.

Some adults attribute their partner's communication failures to a lack of skill and recognize that their partner wanted to be supportive, while others attribute lack of communication to the partner's self-centeredness. Of course, many spouses are simply continuing a relationship-long pattern of interaction. Dissatisfaction with these patterns becomes more salient during the period of bereavement, a time in which need is high and disappointment more acutely felt.

Men may have trouble requesting emotional support because they are often discouraged from expressing emotion and asking for help. For instance, Bobby is disappointed that his wife has not given him more support, but he recognizes that he does not encourage it:

I mean a part of it is you just don't expect support and part of it is not admitting weakness. It's just all of those things that work against men being particularly verbal or communicative.... Men don't cry. That's one of the classics. A lot of men deal with stress by working or just doing other things. [*Interviewer:* Have you felt pressure to be strong?] Oh yeah. I mean I hate to cry.

Bobby is following in his father's footsteps. Bobby describes his father as "a typical American male who was not forthcoming about problems. You know, if his foot was cut off, he'd say, 'Aw, I'll take care of it, it's really okay.' . . . I sort of grew up modeling on him so a lot of times I wouldn't talk to him about problems." Bobby's inability to ask for help reflects the influence of society and socialization. It also reflects personal change following the loss of a parent. Bobby, like many men, identifies more strongly with his father since his father died. Becoming more similar to his father means becoming even more stoic and inexpressive.

When husbands are uncomfortable with the strong expression of emotion that accompanies loss, wives cannot express their feelings or have their needs met. For example, Rebecca, who eventually left her husband, was keenly disappointed in her husband's inability to let her express herself emotionally:

> I wanted him to hold me when I needed to be held and I wanted him to let me cry. Rather than say, "Well, don't break down, don't let it take over you, that's not going to solve anything. . . . You just have to be tough." That's how he's dealt with everything in his life. It was impossible for him to understand that I could not deal with it that way. I had to cry. . . . I know he didn't want to see me suffer, but he felt helpless to help me. He didn't know how to help me.

Bereaved men, on the other hand, often want to avoid the emotions that lie just beneath the surface. These men want a limited kind of support from their partners, yet they want to know the support is available if they need it.

Steven, thirty-six, felt distant from his father, but emphasizes that he always honored his father by being obedient: "The first criteria [sic] is we had to be good boys – basically obedient – good job, good education, buy a house, get a wife, make kids."

Being obedient also meant that Steven had to repress any feelings, thoughts, and emotions that might upset his father:

> I haven't cried since I was a kid. I feel a tightness in my chest sometimes. . . . When my dad died my mother went hysterical . . . but I could see myself standing away from it. You know, I had my shield up. . . . I was trying to protect myself from not getting hurt with the extra emotions.

Steven's wife has adapted to their relationship in a way that makes Steven feel supported from a distance:

> She was trying to support me, gave me lots of hugs and we held hands a lot and stuff like that. . . . The best thing she did was just being there. Asking me if I'm okay.

It is usually easier for partners to hold back emotion, as Mark wanted his wife to do, than it is for partners who are not comfortable with emotion to be open in dealing with a loved one's feelings. In this respect, it may be less difficult for expressive women to support their inexpressive husbands than it is for inexpressive men to support expressive wives. Moreover, individuals who find it easy to be emotionally supportive may be more attuned to the emotional needs of others and may more readily recognize when their grieving partner needs some distance.

Desiring Empathy

Lack of understanding and empathy from others can create a feeling of isolation and loneliness, especially when the bereaved adult is already very upset. Michael has been very depressed since the death of his parents. He has insomnia, anxiety attacks, and nightmares. He is disturbed by his wife's lack of empathy:

> One bad dream is that Daddy's gotten out of his grave and he says, "Michael, everything's going to be okay." He's trying to dig Mama's grave up.... I would get up in the middle of the night and my heart's beating a hundred miles an hour and my mouth is drying up and I made my wife wake up and she got mad.... She has no comprehension of what I'm going through.

Quite a few of the adults I talked with felt that it was impossible for any individual who has not yet been through such a loss to understand the meaning of the loss. As one grieving woman told me, "people that haven't gone through it – they can't know."

It is particularly difficult for the spouse to be empathic when he or she views the deceased parent as an unlikable and perhaps even abusive person. In these cases, as fifty-three-year-old Lynn illustrates, the spouse may feel compelled to point out the deceased parent's inadequacies.

Lynn recently lost both her mother and father. She was always close to her mother but had a difficult relationship with her father. He was emotionally, and possibly physically, abusive of Lynn's mother. Lynn's husband, Frank, was supportive following her mother's death, but Lynn became very upset with Frank following her father's death:

> Even though there were lots of things about my father that I didn't like and I wasn't especially close to him, he was still my father. I did feel a loss when he died and my

husband was angry about that because he really thought my father was a son of a bitch. So that was kind of hard.

Dating back to childhood, most of us feel a certain tension about others' views of our parents. Children and teenagers may criticize their own parents relentlessly yet feel intense anger if another person, especially someone from outside the family, criticizes this parent. Often, the adult desires social affirmation of the parent from others even when the parent was deeply flawed. One's spouse is the most likely person to provide some kind of affirmation of the parent; however, one's spouse is also very likely to be aware of the parent's flaws. These issues can come to the fore following a parent's death when a bereaved adult is working hard to resolve his or her own past with a difficult parent.

Of course, it also matters to us what our parents think of the person we have chosen as a life partner. Some adults feel compelled to end their relationship with a partner whom the parent never really liked. Stephanie's mother, Diedre, died eight months ago. Stephanie is unhappy with her partner, in part because Stephanie knows that Diedre never really liked her partner:

It didn't help that my mom didn't like my girlfriend. She didn't trust her. It wasn't anything to do with the gay thing. She just did not trust this girl. Mom just thought my girlfriend was using me and stuff. So that didn't help the situation. . . . I did have a lot of bitter feelings towards my girlfriend after the funeral. . . . I never saw her upset even though she told me that she'd go off by herself and get upset, that she didn't want to be upset in front of me because she thought she had to be supportive for me.

So, I don't know....I do love her too but...I think our relationship took a big dive when my mom died.

Even if Stephanie wanted to maintain the relationship with her girlfriend, it would be difficult because Stephanie feels such a strong urge to resolve her old fears that her mother did not really care about her; staying involved with her partner means defying Diedre's opinions and wishes.

Chronic Upset

The marital relationship provides a "backstage" on which individuals can express feelings of loss and grief even if they do not express those feelings at work or to persons outside the family.[3] In this sense, a spouse may be the only person to witness the degree of distress or depression experienced by the bereaved person. Some spouses are unnerved by their partner's continuing grief and depression. Depression in a spouse can lead to negative feelings in the nondepressed spouse and can erode marital quality.[4]

Common symptoms of depression include feeling a lack of pleasure in usual routines, feeling tired, and having trouble performing usual roles. Living with a depressed spouse places many demands on the nondepressed partner. The partner must shoulder more of the usual household and childcare responsibilities and is expected to care for the bereaved person's needs as well.

Michael, forty-one, lost his mother unexpectedly about a year ago. His father died five months later. During those final five months, Michael spent a lot of time caring for his father. He left his home and family behind and drove three hours to spend every weekend caring for his father. This imposed a great deal of strain on his marriage, in part because his wife had to assume most of the responsibilities for their own family.

Michael was unusually devoted to caring for his parents. This devotion dates back to his childhood when his mother was an alcoholic and he had to take care of her. He and his father had a special bond because they often worked together to keep his mother out of trouble. His wife did not understand the underlying motivation for Michael's strong commitment to his father, a commitment that interfered with his commitments to his wife and children.

According to Michael, his wife is now frustrated with his continuing depression seven months after his father's death. Michael quit his job several months ago in an attempt to reduce the stress in his life. The inheritance from his parents is sufficient to support him and his family for about a year, but his wife is very bothered by his inability to work. Michael told me, "She was expecting more of me than I thought she should have." Michael's depression interferes with his ability to work and to fulfill his family responsibilities. His wife picks up the slack and is increasingly angry; at the same time, Michael feels let down by his wife. This tension has taken a toll on their marriage.

A spouse's expectations for recovery often exceed the mourner's experience of recovery. A partner may view the bereaved spouse as becoming a different person because of the depressed person's psychological distress. In part, this has happened in Michael's marriage. Nina fears that this has also happened in her marriage.

Several months after Nina's father was murdered, she carried through with her plans to marry Jim – in part because she knew that her father wanted her to marry Jim. Now she finds that she has trouble having normal interactions with her husband.

Nine feels increasingly distant from Jim and avoids sexual intimacy with him. That she sees her father in Jim is one reason that she married him. This may also exacerbate her lack of interest in sex even while it makes her appreciate Jim more:

> If there was ever somebody cut out of just the same mold as my father, it's Jim. They're so much alike it's just unreal. . . . Just his attitude on life and. . . . Jim's such a positive person. . . . The worst day of my life can just be nuts and he understands. . . . I think he's doing a real good job of it. I find myself having to reassure him all the time that I don't think this is the way it will always be. I certainly hope not. It makes me wonder if I should have married him when I did, that it wasn't fair to him.

Some adults are comforted when they see positive qualities of a much-loved parent in their spouse. However, the sudden and violent nature of Nina's father's death is very painful for her. Seeing her father in her husband only serves to remind Nina of her loss.

Bereaved adults have many emotional needs following a parent's death. In many instances, when these needs become exaggerated in a depressed adult, he or she leans heavily on their partner to replace the emotional sustenance and support that a parent might provide to a child in need. This will almost always be a difficult, if not impossible, role for the partner to fill.

TILL DEATH DO US PART

Several of the adults I interviewed decided to separate or divorce shortly following their parents' death. When I talked with men and women about the reasons for these breakups, they typically told stories characterized by a final disillusionment, a sense of liberation, and/or personal change that was unacceptable to their partner.

The Final Straw

Clearly, for many individuals who separate after the loss of a parent, the strains associated with loss merely provide the final straw needed to end the relationship. The death of a parent is a highly symbolic loss, and a spouse's failure to understand that loss becomes symbolic as well.

Ginger, introduced at the beginning of this book, left a marriage of twelve years after her father died. She left her husband because she wanted to be a happier person, living life to its fullest – a person more like her father. When her husband was not there for her emotionally after her father died, she ended the relationship:

> It was just one more time when Larry wasn't there for me. So it almost gave me a focus to get angry which is what I needed to do to get out of the relationship. . . . Any time I had an emotional need, he wasn't around. . . . Any time that I needed some stability, he didn't want to be the stable influence in my life so he wasn't around. In this case, it was a very positive thing for me. It was like, "Okay, fine, I can do this. Thank you very much." It helped me get on with things.

Rebecca, forty-one, lived in a troubled marriage before her parents died. Her husband's response to her mother's death also crystallized her resolve to leave her marriage:

> It was just a continuation of the way that Darrell had always been. I felt like I tried not to put too many demands

on him. But . . . when we reached that point where I really needed him and I did call on him, he failed me miserably – when I needed him the most.

Rebecca, like Ginger, felt that she could not be herself in her marriage, and this contributed to her marital unhappiness:

I had to get out from under that roof and out of that situation that was clutching. He's just suffocating and strangling me because he doesn't want to lose me. . . . He's always been very possessive, very jealous, very intimidated by my independent nature, which is my true nature. I, in turn, trying to accommodate his sensitivities and feelings . . . would try to stifle my own self and not be independent and try not to do the things that would make him feel more insecure than he did. And in the course of that, I just lost who I was and how I felt.

Rebecca's feelings about her husband paralleled her feelings of oppression and judgment from her parents. Rebecca now feels liberated from both her parents and her husband.

Free at Last

Some bereaved adults leave a marriage after a parent's death partly because they no longer worry about how their parent will view the breakup. The death frees them to make their own decisions and pursue their own course in life.

Rebecca's decision to leave her husband became a possibility only after her parents died. Rebecca is from a strict Pentecostal family where physical discipline of children was frequent and severe. She was the youngest of seven children, and seven years younger than the next older sibling. She, more than her siblings, was sheltered by her parents. As an adult, she moved next door to her parents so that her young daughter could be near her grandparents. But this proximity only perpetuated the lifelong sensation of being monitored by her parents:

> It was obvious when my car was not in the driveway at certain times of the night or something like that and they were just anxious. I would always feel an obligation to let them know when something was going to be taking place out of the ordinary.

After her parents died, Rebecca felt liberated. Rebecca's personal liberation led to divorce and greater happiness:

> Before they died it was still like I had to report in.... I can tell you honestly, if Mom and Dad were still here, I'd probably still be there with my husband. Because of their opinion... their expectations of me and also in my need to be there next to them, for as long as they were living.... It was against their beliefs that a marriage should end in divorce.... But once Mom and Dad were gone, that gave me a lot of freedom. Because I didn't have that sort of subconscious feeling any longer of having to be accountable to them.... I knew that I really didn't have to justify my actions or my lifestyle or anything to my parents.

Rebecca is now free to be herself, to no longer "stifle [her] own self." Her lifelong relationship with her observant and judgmental parents is over. Rebecca married someone who made her feel very much like her parents did. Her parent's death frees her from her parents and from her husband. She can now try to be the independent person she believes herself to be and wants to be. Clearly, parents have a great deal of influence over their adult children throughout life. Losing this influence, in some cases, is liberating to the child.

Left Behind

Personal change in the bereaved adult may also motivate the nonbereaved partner to leave the relationship. This happened to Paula, thirty-six, who always felt closer to her father than to her mother:

> My father was born in 1908 and so when I came along he was forty-eight years old.... When I was little I could go climb in his lap. He was not overly demonstrative but I was. It was like I was allowed to be there.... He was my ally because my mother was like the drill sergeant.... We didn't talk about things. He would take me to the movies on Sunday afternoon but he would say, "Don't tell Mother but we'll go get ice cream."

Paula nurtured this special secret relationship with her father even after he died, and this relationship directly contributed to Paula's divorce. Paula grew up in a conservative Christian home that was led by her mother. It was only after her father died that Paula learned her father was Jewish. Paula's personal identity is now strongly linked to being Jewish like her father. This change in self-identity is, of course, a way of revering her father, holding on to him and honoring him:

> It was not discussed that Daddy was a Jew. I've asked mother point-blank and she will admit to me that he was

a Jew but he was not practicing. . . . In her way of running the family, she kept a lot of information away from me. . . . I've only recently been able to put these pieces together. . . . When I went to the Christian College at eighteen, I tried to witness to my father because this was how the college was programming me. He said to me, "Honey, I have my own religion." . . . Why didn't I say, "Well, what is it?" . . . Since he died, I've converted to Judaism. . . . The first rabbi I worked with said, . . . "I think you are just trying to connect to your father and there is nothing else here." . . . [*Interviewer*: If you hadn't found out that he was Jewish, would you have followed this path?] . . . I probably would not have been as motivated or felt as comfortable. . . . I felt I had some reason, some family connection, to be there.

Paula keeps this part of her life, her conversion to Judaism, a secret from her mother just as she and her father used to keep the ice cream a secret. Paula says, "I think my father would be very happy and there would be kind of a smirk on his face meaning, 'You outsmarted your mother.'" Through her conversion, Paula continues a relationship with her father and experiences a seismic shift in self-identity. In addition to her conversion and her active participation in the local Jewish community, Paula is more motivated than ever to settle down and have children, to create her own Jewish family. Paula was married at the time of her father's death, but not to a Jewish man. All of the personal changes in Paula – her religious conversion and her sudden emphatic desire to have children – led her husband to seek a divorce. As Paula puts it, her husband "freaked out" over the changes in her. Since the divorce, Paula has dated several Jewish men and hopes she can have children in the near future.

THE BEST IS YET TO BE

The national survey shows that a decline in marital quality is much more likely than improvement in marital quality following a parent's death. However, not all couples experience diminished marital quality following a parent's death. A look at those couples offers insight into marriages that do well, even becoming closer, following a parent's death.

What characterizes those couples who experience their relationships in a positive way following a life crisis? First and foremost, these couples began with a solid foundation that can withstand a stressful event. In addition, they tend to interact in certain characteristic ways that help the bereaved person. A partner may be very supportive and feel a sense of shared loss, or the bereaved person may understand and accept the partner's abilities (or inabilities) to provide support. These positive features of relationships virtually mirror the negative experiences that characterize marriages in decline.

To Love and Cherish

As I suggested earlier, some supportive spouses cannot seem to do enough or provide exactly the right kind of support to their bereaved partner; in such cases, the marriage may suffer. In marriages that thrive following the loss, the bereaved adult often recognizes and appreciates the supportive efforts of his or her spouse, even when the bereaved adult desires more support or a different kind of support. That is, the bereaved spouse is able to maintain a benevolent view of his or her partner even in the face of extreme need.

Desley, fifty-three, lost her seventy-five-year-old mother six months before our interview. This was a painful loss for Desley, and her husband was an important supporter after her mother's death:

> My husband has been very understanding. . . . He is a person that doesn't express emotion very easily. . . . But he was able to allow me to express grief. I think the main thing was he was there. He went with me to the nursing home when she died. He went with me to the funeral home to help arrange the funeral. He was with me during the funeral. He was with me afterwards. You know, every step of the way he was there, physically with me. I mean it was the greatest thing. . . . I think it would have been helpful if he would have been able to express his sadness at my mother's death. We had been married almost thirty years, so there was a strong relationship between him and my mother. But he wasn't able to do that even for his own father's death. It's just something he's not comfortable with.

Desley accepts the differences between herself and her husband; this acceptance is a key to success in marriages generally. Of course, she has a husband who, in spite of their differences, found many ways to demonstrate his support for her. Importantly, he also allowed her to express her grief even while he was uncomfortable expressing his own.

The Tasks of Living

Bereaved adults often value the spouse who is willing to help out with routine tasks and responsibilities as well as with the tasks involved around funerals and estate settlements. The social and practical chores associated with the death can be quite stressful.

Sharon's mother died two and a half years ago. Her mother suffered from cancer for the last two years of her life and spent her last month in Sharon's home. Sharon married twenty-two years ago, and according to her, the marriage has had its share of ups and downs, including a period of dealing with her husband's alcoholism. Sharon says that her husband was an incredible source of support during her mother's illness and after her death. He willingly invited Sharon's mother to spend her last weeks in their home and he helped care for her while she was ill. Sharon feels closer to her husband than ever before. Much of the respect and love she feels for her husband results from his unwavering help in taking care of their mentally and physically disabled daughter. This enabled Sharon to help her mother and to recover from her mother's death: "My husband was the best support ever. Because he concentrated on caring for our daughter so much of the time. . . . He was the best support ever and still is."

Sharon views her mother as a teacher, a person who guided her through life with good advice and wisdom. Near the end of her life, Sharon's mother emphasized to Sharon that it is very important to take time each day to focus on communicating with her husband. Sharon took this advice to heart and feels that she and her husband are closer because of it.

Shared Loss and the Parent in the Partner

In my conversations with adults whose marriages actually improved following the loss, the bereaved often told me that they felt a special tie to their partner when the partner also cared about the parent who died.

Michelle, thirty-eight, has felt a great sense of loss since her father died thirteen months ago. It means a lot to Michelle that her husband loved her father and that her husband is so much like her father:

> He was really sad, weeping at the funeral. He really liked my father. In fact, my husband read something at the funeral. He said my father was a character and there aren't many characters left in the world. He really respected my father because my father's ethics were to be admired. And Joel, my husband, is real ethical too and there are so many people who aren't ethical nowadays. My father was always helping us and showing us things. Joel's a real project person too, a hands-on type of person. So he and my father spent a lot of time talking. He really respected my father.... I think I appreciate my husband more, because you realize that anybody can go at anytime.... I think deep down, I certainly appreciate him more.

Some individuals, such as Michelle, see more of the parent in their spouse, perhaps more than they realized prior to the loss. This keeps the parent alive and involved in an ongoing relationship with the bereaved adult. Some adults want their spouse to assume their deceased parent's old roles. This is a difficult role to fill and is often too much to ask of the nonbereaved spouse. This situation can contribute to marital strain, even leading to rejection of the partner. On the other hand, some bereaved adults find that, at least in limited ways, if their spouse assumes some parental-like qualities, it is comforting and makes the marriage closer.

Jackie, thirty-six, was only ten years old when her mother died. Her much-loved father was eighty-one when he died only a little over a year ago:

> My father was an atypical man. He single-handedly raised me after my mother died. He cooked meals and provided

a nontraditional upbringing for me in a small town. I was fiercely defensive of him whenever he was criticized by traditional thinkers. He was independent of spirit and a tremendously fun, garrulous person. People took to him instantly. What I have lost is that kind and loving presence, his pretty much unconditional love and support.

Jackie's husband was also close to her father. The sense that her husband shares this loss with her has helped her to cope with the loss and to feel closer to her husband. In addition, she sees some of her father's qualities in her husband:

The important and loving help I got from my husband was a direct result of how much he admired and loved my dad. My siblings whose spouses weren't wild about Dad seem to be having a different experience. I think if you and your spouse are really tuned in to one another, how the spouse feels about the lost parent is crucial. If my husband had disliked my father it would have been a whole different scenario – less support, more difficult for me to cope. I see in my husband more of my father's traits – both good and bad! They were always there. They just seem more pronounced now.

CONCLUSION

The death of a parent places strain on most marital relationships. Declining marital quality typically occurs because the partner fails to provide emotional support; the partner cannot comprehend the significance and meaning of the loss; or the partner is disappointed in the bereaved adult's ability to recover quickly. Some partners feel imposed on by continuing distress and depression in the be- reaved person, especially when they have to shoulder the usual roles and responsibilities of the bereaved adult.

The grieving partner often has a new and greater need for support from his or her spouse following the death of a parent. Marital decline is due, in part, to the bereaved adult's attempt to compensate for the lost parent. The idealized image of a parent is that of a person who unfailingly provides just the right amount of unconditional emotional support when the child needs it. Once the parent dies, whether or not he or she actually fulfilled the fantasy of the all-loving parent, adults feel the loss of a unique source of support; sometimes that loss is literal and other times it is symbolic. The loss may be even more poignant if the adult child never actually received the love that he or she needed from a parent: The loss only highlights that that love will now never be forthcoming. Bereaved adults often turn to their spouse to meet these support needs and end up feeling disappointed in their spouse's inability or unwillingness to fill this role. The spouse may feel, quite fairly, that they cannot or will not replace the bereaved partner's parent.

Personal change is the hallmark of parental loss in adulthood. Adults experience change in their psychological well-being, roles and responsibilities, priorities in life, and attitudes and values. Personal change in the bereaved adult can lead to far-reaching change in marital relationships. In some cases the adult decides to live life more fully, to be more like the vibrant lost parent – and living life more fully can mean leaving a spouse. In other cases the adult decides to adopt the deceased parent's religion and a new cultural identity, and to start having children in this new framework – these changes can "freak out" the partner, who then seeks a divorce. Most personal changes and changes in a marriage reflect the bereaved adult's past with his or her parent and the ways that the adult is coming to terms with the loss. Significant change in a spouse upsets the usual balance in a marriage and requires both partners to alter their usual interactions with one another. Many marriages do not adapt well to these changes.

An important minority of marriages seems to improve in quality following the loss of a parent. An emotionally supportive and empathic spouse can make the bereaved adult feel much loved and can facilitate recovery from the loss. In many cases, the bereaved adult sees positive qualities of the lost parent in his or her spouse and begins to appreciate the spouse even more than before. Unfortunately, following a parent's death, positive change is much less likely to occur than negative change in marriages.

Family systems theorists emphasize the complex balance of individuals' needs and abilities within a family, and the need for a family to maintain a kind of equilibrium over time. A death in the family disrupts the existing equilibrium in a family, and a new balance must be achieved. The death affects each person in the family differently, but each person's reactions reflect the needs and reactions of others in the family.[5] In this way, all relationships in the family are altered by the death. In this chapter, we have seen that a parent's death has profound consequences – usually negative – for marital relationships; however, a parent's death does not affect all family relationships in the same way. In the next chapter, we explore how a parent's death affects relationships with children.

6

THE NEXT GENERATION

My kids were taking care of me. . . . I didn't realize they had such good skills. . . . That was kind of a revelation.

HELEN, AGE FIFTY-TWO

I am what survives me.

ERIK ERIKSON, IDENTITY: YOUTH AND CRISIS [1]

The death of a parent highlights the reality of our own individual mortality, especially since it is most likely to occur in middle adulthood, when our concerns about death are already on the rise. The death of a parent is about the end of one generation and the passing of a torch to the next generation. As we receive that torch, we become more focused on our own children. We consider the meaning of our relationships with our sons and daughters and what kind of personal legacy might be passed into the future through our children.

Erik Erikson was one of the first psychologists to argue that human development extends beyond childhood and even into old age. Erikson saw middle adulthood as being loosely linked to the seventh stage of human life when the key issue for individuals is generativity. Generativity refers to "a concern for and commitment to the next generation."[2] Erikson argued that during this stage of life, adults must resolve the conflict between self-interest and contributing to society and the next generation.

According to Erikson, having and rearing children can foster generativity. It is about nurturance and responsible caring for others, about a preoccupation with something outside the self. Achieving generativity may result in the furthering of adult maturation, but, as therapist Kathy Kotre contends, generativity is also about a focus on the self – about a "desire to invest one's substance in forms of life and work that will outlive the self." Although literal immortality cannot be achieved, generativity is a way to ensure one's "symbolic immortality."[3] Generativity is also central to much of the change in adult identity that occurs following a parent's death.

The death of a parent is a symbolic loss that affects views of self, one's children, and one's philosophy of parenting. Resulting changes in the way in which one thinks can alter the dynamics and quality of parent-child relationships. The death is also a stressful life event. At a time when the bereaved person may already be experiencing distress as a result of parent loss, a positive relationship with one's own children can alleviate some of the adult's distress, while difficulties with a child can exacerbate the distress associated with loss.

Overall, the results from the national survey suggest a positive picture of how relationships with older children (that is, those aged sixteen and older) fare following the loss.[4] Yet the death of a parent affects relationships between parents and younger children in a different way. In fact, adults who have minor children are likely to experience parenting as even more demanding and burdensome than they did before the loss. This is probably because such parents must continue to cope with the daily demands of parenting young children even while they must sort out how to deal with their own grief and loss.

Children aged sixteen and older actually increase the amount of emotional support they give to their parents after the parent loses his or her mother or father. Older children who live independently begin to visit with their parent more often following the death of the grandparent, but this increase in emotional support from children and frequency of contact with older children gradually diminishes over the first thirty-six months following bereavement. This suggests that although older children rally to a parent's side following the loss, this rally is most active in the first few months after the death. Of course, the period immediately following the death is likely to be when the bereaved person is experiencing the greatest need for contact and support from others. Interviews with the bereaved also show that although the actual support and visiting may diminish over time, important changes in the relationship – particularly in how the parent perceives the child – are more enduring.

CLOSER RELATIONSHIPS WITH CHILDREN

Most adults say that they feel closer to their own children after a parent dies. This often occurs because parents and children share a sense of grief and loss.

Lynn has two adult sons. Her younger son was close to his grandmother and sharing this loss has brought them closer together: "My younger son, the twenty-six-year-old, has really experienced a lot of grief and he and I have been able to talk about that and to share our feelings with each other – and some memories about [my mother]. I think that it has been helpful to both of us."

Many adults believe that no one except a sibling or a child can appreciate the loss because these are the only people who knew and cared as much about the deceased parent as did the bereaved adult.

Lois and her son, who was fifteen at the time of her father's death, grew closer after their loss, partly because her son had a more positive relationship with his grandfather than Lois had with her father:

> I think we're a little bit closer. . . . Josh was the son my father never had since there were four daughters. . . . We talk a lot more. We talk about Grandpa a lot because Josh was real close to him. He didn't see the kind of things I saw growing up. Grandpa was everything to him. . . . At Christmas they used to hand out the presents together. The day before Christmas, Josh said, "Mom, I don't think I can deal with it." And I said, "Why?" And he said, "Grandpa's not going to be here and Christmas isn't going to be the same." Josh just admitted to me two weeks ago that he cried himself to sleep for the first three months after Grandpa died.

Lois is still coming to terms with her difficult childhood, so it is helpful to her to focus on the positive aspects of her father and to see her father through her son's eyes; this refocusing helps her to reframe who her father was and feel a bit more resolution of that relationship.

ROLE REVERSAL

Bereaved adults may see the first glimmer of role reversal in the relationship with an older son or daughter when the child begins to offer support and comfort to the bereaved. This happened to Helen, who has four adult children.

Helen's parents divorced when she was fifteen, and from that time until Helen began to have children of her own, she was not terribly close to her father: "When I was having children, I started feeling closer to him again. . . . I started thinking about my parents in a different way. . . . I had more of an understanding of who they were as people. I could identify with them more as parents."

Helen's children, two sons and two daughters, range in age from twenty-five to thirty-five. She is impressed by the new role that her children play in relation to her:

> My kids were magnificent. They were at their finest. . . .
> I mean it's either constant phone communication . . . or
> physical contact. . . . They know what I need. . . . They un-
> derstand me. . . . That was a very beautiful part of this.
> I thought, look at this, they are so grown up, they're so
> great. The roles changed. This is the first big crisis where
> I became aware of them taking care of me.

The death may even motivate a troubled child to change in a positive direction. One of Adam's greatest losses following the death of his seriously ill father was the dissolution of the extended family. Adam was surprised that his extended family seemed to fall apart, and he is now equally surprised that he and his son are closer:

> I have a problem son, twenty-three years old. He has done
> drugs, time in jail, and is unemployed most of the time.
> Since my father died – he was close to his Grandpa – he
> has pretty much stayed out of trouble and really seems to
> understand my position as his father. He shows much more
> respect for me now.

LINKING GENERATIONS

One consolation for the bereaved is the belief that the parent lives on in the child and that legacies are passed along from their parents into the future. Bobby, forty-one, an only child, is more focused now than ever before on the linkages between three generations: "The loss of my dad is something to share with my son. You begin to look at legacies and passing things along. . . . I kind of knew that already but it brought it into focus."

Bereaved adults may take comfort in the knowledge that their parent and child got to know one another before the death. While her parents were alive, Rebecca made a real effort to bring her parents and daughter close together:

> It was my primary objective to have my daughter, Sarah, be there so that she could know them . . . on a daily basis be-cause I felt so robbed of that with my own grandparents. . . . After my dad passed away, Sarah would go up every morn-ing and eat breakfast with my mom before she went to school. Even before my dad passed away . . . she would usu-ally stop in to feed the birds with them. . . . Sarah would help him in the garden. She spent quite a bit of time with him and they had a real good relationship and I'm so thankful for that.

Many of the bereaved wish that they had done more to doc-ument their parents' and family's history. Rebecca regrets not collecting more information from her parents:

> We kept saying we were going to sit down with a tape recorder and make Dad sit down and tape all of his

stories – his fascinating stories about working on the railroad, . . . cutting timber in the Smokies. . . . I mean, we have such a rich ancestry with our folks. . . . It was wonderful and all of us just loved Daddy and his stories and his tales. All that's lost, because we never bothered to record it.

Rebecca regrets not having more formal documentation of her parents' history, but she is passing along the family stories in the oral tradition. Rebecca, like many bereaved children, is finding her own unique ways of documenting the past:

My mother saved things that I drew or wrote . . . things that you don't realize when you're doing them, but they were just precious to her. . . . Going through and sorting through all of their affairs and all their possessions and all of that is just so special. You can't keep your parents with you forever, but you can have those little reminders. . . . Like when my father was in the Navy . . . we found a whole stack of little letters tied up in little ribbons that he had sent home to Mom. . . . You go back and you think, I never knew my dad talked about me like that – "To my precious little baby darling daughter, your loving Da-da and kiss your sweet Mama for me."

Even when the deceased parent knew his or her grandchildren, bereaved adults are often sad that the older and younger generations did not have more time together. Patty's sixty-six-year-old mother died of breast cancer about a year ago. She has two children, ages four and five:

The hardest thing about losing my mom is my kids. They didn't get a chance to know my mom as well as I would have wanted them to know her. When she died, they lost the person for whom they could never do anything wrong. . . . Some of the hardest things are . . . special times I know my mother would really like to have heard about . . . like when my son went to the first day of school.

Patty's sadness is about not having a mother to share her children with, about the loss of a grandparent for her children, and about her mother's lost opportunity to experience grandparenting. The loss of a parent is about the connected losses of three generations.

The link between a grandparent and grandchild is symbolic to the middle generation. As Chapter 2 shows, feelings of generativity can even promote recovery and psychological well-being following a parent's death.

CONCERNED PARENTS

Losing a parent, especially a younger parent, can leave the bereaved feeling more vulnerable. As a result, many adults begin to worry more about their children. A sense of vulnerability along with increasing recognition of personal mortality leads most adults to be more concerned about how their own death will someday affect their child. Marta, age forty, told me, "I think a lot about what my death will be like for my son."

The concern over one's own death partly reflects adults' new and poignant personal recognition of the degree of loss that is attached to the death of a parent. The bereaved find it difficult to avoid thinking of their own eventual death when faced with the irrefutable evidence that parents do die and children do lose their parents. The recognition of personal mortality is at the foundation of a new focus on generational linkages and legacies.

Confrontation with death and mortality leaves adults feeling vulnerable and this affects their relationships with children. Joan lost both parents over a three-day period. The deaths were completely unexpected: Her mother died of a heart attack as she slept; her father had a stroke shortly after discovering his wife's body and died three days later:

> I feel closer to my children now. Life is more precious now than it's ever been. I find that I am always worrying about my children. I have become somewhat paranoid. Since Mom and Dad died so suddenly, I'm petrified something else will happen. . . . If my son is late getting home, I imagine all sorts of things happening.

Joan's losses and new sense of vulnerability led to a reordering of priorities in her life, "I believe I have more love of family. I've come to accept our mortality. . . . My family is my number one priority now. Before, I was juggling job and family. Now there is no contest."

Bereaved adults often worry about their child's response to the loss. Many of these children are learning about death for the first time and they may become anxious about the possibility of losing their own parent.

Sandy is one of those people whose life improved following her father's death. She decided to live life fully and happily just as her father had. She left a troubled marriage and moved to a new city. She is a happier person now than she was before but she worries about one of her daughters:

> Dad was a big part of my girls' life. He was more of a father to them than their natural father. They spent a great deal of time with him. It has brought us closer together to share this loss. But my younger daughter has had severe emotional problems coupled with drug and alcohol abuse and I think dad's illness and death, our moving, and divorce all in one year were responsible for these problems. It was hard to help her when I was so sad. She is much better now and we are closer for having gone through it.

Parents worry that their own grief interferes with caring for their child. This is especially likely in families with younger children and this worry may add to the usual strains of parenting. Tina, for example, worries about her eight-year-old daughter:

> I worried about her trying to take on adult roles and take care of me because I did a lot of that when I was a child. . . . I am more needy over the last few months than I have ever been in her short life. So she has tried to take care of me a lot and I worry about that and I try to discourage that but I also wonder if that's her way of coping with it because she said she couldn't cry. . . . I'm trying to be more mindful about where she is with this, if she's trying to take care of me. If my husband and I get into a heated discussion, she tries to intervene and smooth things over. I saw myself doing that same thing when I was a kid. And I want to turn that around.

Tina's concern is sharpened by her own past. Her father was a violent and unpredictable man who mistreated Tina's mother. Tina spent a lifetime trying to console her parents and reduce the strain between them. As her parents grew older, she played an active role in caring for them. Even until the time of her father's death, Tina worried about him: "Over the last year, I was trying to provide support and strength to him more than vice versa. He really needed it. He was very needy emotionally." In fact, Tina got little back from her parents, even as a child. Tina sees her own daughter behaving much as she did as a child and she wants to break this cycle for her daughter. In essence, she wants to discontinue generational linkages that she sees as painful and dysfunctional.

PARENTING STRATEGIES

A parent's death sometimes leads adults to alter their own parenting strategies. Individuals who had a positive relationship with a parent often want to become more like him or her when dealing with their children. Richard greatly admired his father, who always made Richard feel loved and supported:

> We were able to talk a great deal before his death.... He died bravely and showed a personal strength that made me proud.... Like always, he tried to make it easier for *me*.

Richard is trying to be a better father to his children, more like the father he had: "I told my dad on his deathbed that I have never been as patient with my kids as he was with me and I would try to do better."

Others, typically those who had a troubled relationship with a parent, want to avoid being like him or her. Lynn, the woman who feels that she grew closer to her younger son because the two of them shared so many feelings around her mother's death, is not very close to her older son, yet she tries to treat her sons in a very even-handed way. This strong emphasis on equal treatment of children is more important to Lynn now that she reflects on the past with her parents:

> My husband and I helped the older son with the down payment on a house. I've just begun to mull over a lot of things like that. My parents were not very even-handed in what they gave materially to their three children. I know there were reasons for it. You always want to give more to the one that needs it the most or that you think needs it the most. But I'm not sure that's always the wisest course. It's made me think a lot about how I want to do that kind of thing with my children. It's hurtful when things are not even and I want to make sure that I give more fairly.

Certainly, some of the bereaved reflect on their past and use this information to consciously direct change in relationships with their own children. Mark's father never expressed any love or pride in Mark, and this history now guides his relationship with his own children. Mark's pain of wishing for affirmation from his father has only increased since the loss. Mark has two children, ages fifteen and twenty-one, and he is making conscious decisions about parenting his older children in an effort to avoid his father's mistakes: "I wanted to make sure that my children wouldn't look back and wish I had told them I loved them or that I was proud of them."

Some individuals reevaluate their parenting role, placing a higher priority on their children and family relationships. Until her alcoholic father died, Lois was an exceedingly driven and busy woman. In part, her frenetic lifestyle kept her from focusing on the difficulties with her childhood and her father. After her father died, Lois turned her life around. She quit a high-powered job and decided it was time to focus on her fifteen-year-old son:

> I was too busy, too wrapped up in work and I didn't even watch my son grow up because, I mean, I was so busy working so many hours, keeping up with the Joneses, making more and more money, that when I finally quit I realized that Luke was almost grown up. And it was like, "Wow, I started at the company when he was two and a half years old?" I feel like I missed a lot. So I almost tried to make up for it now. And now, of course, he's almost eighteen so he really doesn't want me around. It's like, "Come on Mom, get a life."

Lois jokes about Luke not needing her, but she feels that he appreciates having her at home and she knows that they have grown closer since she quit her job. Lois has managed to resolve a lot of old issues with her father since his death. Making her family a higher priority was contrary to what her father had always done, and it has helped Lois to move forward and feel that she is contributing something important – something more important than making money.

A STEADYING INFLUENCE

Parents of young children are more likely than nonparents to feel a sense of obligation and responsibility to stay well.[5] They tend to take better care of their health than do other adults. Research shows that parents have lower mortality rates than nonparents, especially from causes of death that include some behavioral component, such as, alcoholism, car accidents, or suicide.[6] I saw this steadying influence of young children in my interviews with bereaved adults.

Having to be available for young children may lead adults to suppress self-destructive behavior. For instance, young children, out of their own vulnerability and dependence, may jolt a very depressed parent away from suicidal impulses.

Michael feels that his parents loved him unconditionally, that they were perfect parents who could do no wrong – even though his mother was an alcoholic and his father could never fully protect Michael from his mother's collapses. Michael has trouble reconciling his idealized image of his parents with some very painful and lonely experiences in his life. He is seriously depressed, even to the point of considering suicide:

> I don't ever quit thinking about my parents. . . . My wife went to Dallas to see her dad. And I got so depressed and scared during that time that I really thought about suicide. . . . I was absolutely scared to death because my two little boys need me.

One of the few joys Michael can find through his grief is his sons, now seven and nine. Although Michael has lost interest in

most activities and quit his job, he remains involved in his sons'
lives:

> I've got two little boys and they are the light of my life. . . .
> I've always been very, very close with my children. We
> hug a lot and talk a lot. . . . And I do everything that I can
> do with them and participate in their sports events and
> whatever and that helps me tremendously.

Similarly, Susan feels a tremendous sense of loss following the
death of her mother. She expects that she will never fully recover,
yet her three young sons – nine-year-old twins and a seven-year-
old – help to keep her afloat:

> At first, I thought I was going to die. I thought, "Well,
> Mama is gone, I don't want to live much longer.". . . Forty
> years after my mother's mother died, she still missed her.
> She'd just start crying. I love my mother the same way
> so I know it will be hard for me. . . . I remember thinking
> before – that when mom died I would probably kill myself
> because I wouldn't want to live. But I can't do that. I have
> my little boys to think of.

Susan is weathering this loss and making many changes in her
life. She has returned to school and is the new matriarch in her
extended family. She also sees some change in the relationship
with her sons:

> This loss doesn't make me a better mother. Well, maybe a
> little bit. But it makes my love for my boys stronger. . . . I
> don't care what they turn out to be. I want to be there for

them. . . . I also think it makes me more likely to protect them till death or something like that. . . . I might have before but now I think about it and I know I would go that far.

In part, Susan feels protective of her sons in their interactions with her husband, their stepfather. Susan's father was abusive when she was a child. Her own mother was unable to protect her from her father. Susan protects her sons as she needed to be protected long ago. In this way, Susan has begun to resolve some of her own childhood issues.

Taking care of children's daily needs may require the bereaved adult to stick with a schedule and stay busy. This, in and of itself, is helpful to some adults. David's mother committed suicide two months ago. David is divorced and has custody of his four-year-old son, Eli. Taking care of Eli was the saving grace for David in the aftermath of his mother's death:

> I just continued the schedule with him. . . . He was good for me because he didn't know what was going on and he was real happy and upbeat. . . . Eli just went on as if nothing happened. . . . I feel like we're a lot closer. He's only four years old. . . . It just seems like we've done more together. I probably interact with him more. . . . I just feel like he's gotten cheated too because he's not going to have a grandma around.

Since his mother's death, David is feeling that life is more fragile and loved ones are more vulnerable. This changed world view is partly responsible for David's greater involvement with Eli:

> I'm just more aware that life could be taken away at any time. Whereas in the past maybe I thought I was invincible

and it might not happen for a long time. I could control it. Sometimes you can't. Things just happen.

Some parents worry about hiding their feelings of despair from young children. Ella, thirty-six, is concerned that her own distress upsets her young daughters, ages two and four:

> I try not to let the girls see me cry very much because . . .
> I didn't want them to see how upset I was, to think that
> death is a bad thing. . . . There have been times that I have
> cried and [my four-year-old] says, "Mommy, are you sad?"
> and I say "Yeah," and she goes, "Are you thinking about
> Grandma? I miss her too." I don't want her to feel like she
> has to cry.

NEGATIVE INVOLVEMENT

Although most bereaved adults experience improved relationships with their children, some have problems with certain children that make it more difficult for them to recover from the loss of a parent.

Many parents have at least one child with whom they have a troubled relationship. Sometimes a child has emotional and personal problems that are unrelated to the grandparent's death, and such troubled relationships with children reduce the bereaved person's strength to cope with loss.

Kit's father died unexpectedly two years ago, and the loss shattered her outlook on life and family:

> I feel so lost. It's hard to describe. The whole family –
> myself and my brothers and sisters – also feel like it was just

a bad dream and we'll wake up. . . . It's like an important part of your life just ended. You no longer can turn to him for advice, jokes, or anything else again.

Kit feels closer to her husband, siblings, and one of her children than she did before her father died. But her teenage son has made it more difficult to cope:

I seem to have problems with my son now and dealing with him. He went through some behavioral problems after his grandfather and grandmother died and I was in no shape to deal with it.

Similarly, Jenna faced difficulties dealing with her children following her father's death. At the time of her father's death almost a year ago, Jenna's children were sixteen, twelve, and eight:

I feel like my children suffered a lot because of me caring for both my parents. I never had time to go shopping, go to a movie, go eat lunch with them at school, just talk, or even take them anywhere out of town for very long without an act of Congress. My oldest is very rebellious. She's a straight-A student, doesn't sleep around, drink or do drugs, but we argue constantly. She is very angry inside and I don't have the money or insurance to take her to a counselor and she probably wouldn't go, but I worry about her. I wonder if she hates me as much as she says. I doubt it though. My middle child is a typical want-to-please-everyone child. She has more trouble with grades. . . . She misses Mama and Daddy the most. She writes stories about them all the time – too much I'm afraid. My youngest, a boy, is a normal nine-year-old. Does well in school. Talks too much, loves to torment his sisters, but is a real joy to me.

Chronic strains of parenting and a busy life can make it more difficult to recover from the loss of a parent.

CONCLUSION

A parent's death affects one's relationships with teens and older children in a very different way than it affects relationships with younger children. A parent's grief can interfere with the performance of usual responsibilities and with the quality of interactions with young children. Depression in a parent may cause behavioral and psychological problems for young children. Children's problems may only exacerbate the parent's depression and feelings of being overwhelmed. The loss holds special meaning for adults with young children because the opportunity is lost for children to ever really know the grandparent or for the grandparent to know the child. Parents may have to help a young child cope with the first loss of a known and valued person. On the other hand, having to care for children sometimes keeps adults from falling too deeply into their own grief.

Older children are more aware of the significance of the parent's loss. This often leads them to be more supportive of the grieving parent. Older children have had more opportunities to get to know their grandparent, so that the loss may be painful for the grandchild as well as the adult child. The parent and child may share the loss and, through sharing, grow closer to one another. Older children are more likely to assume household tasks that the parent usually performs and to provide care and support to their bereaved parent. Changing parent/child roles lead parents to see their children in a new light and to see themselves as growing older.

Relationships with children, unlike marital relationships, are more likely to improve than to deteriorate after a parent's death. Yet, like marital relationships, change in relationships with children is often linked to the bereaved adult's life history – to the childhood and adult experiences with the parent who died. Depending on the past, adults may feel compelled to emulate or to avoid the parent's child-rearing strategies. Again, the past is carried into the future.

7

THE PARENT LEFT BEHIND

I feel like I have to look out for my mother....My dad always took care of everything. Now she calls me and sometimes I don't know what to do.   LORRIE. AGE THIRTY-TWO

She grieves for him a lot of the time. I call her up and she's crying and wishing that he was here and that's kind of hard.
     ALEJANDRO. AGE THIRTY-ONE

S tress researchers place the death of a spouse at the top of the list when ranking the severity of stressful life events. Widowhood can undermine mental health and physical health, and even contribute to mortality. Widowed women are 27 percent more likely than married women of the same age to die, whereas widowed men are 47 percent more likely than married men of the same age to die.[1] In addition to the psychological toll the death of a spouse can bring on, the deceased spouse may also have played a role in monitoring the spouse's health and in providing medical treatment and assistance to him or her. These factors contribute to the higher mortality rates of the widowed as compared with the married.

Women are much more likely than men to lose a spouse. Among sixty-five- to seventy-four-year-olds, 39 percent of women and 9 percent of men are widowed; among those aged seventy-five and older, 67 percent of women and 23 percent of men are widowed.[2] Both widowed men and women often have new needs following a spouse's death, and adult children may be called on or feel responsible for meeting those needs.

People generally perceive the loss of a spouse to be a much more significant loss than an adult's loss of a parent. Thus, the bereaved adult may feel that his or her needs and emotions are secondary to those of the surviving parent. Furthermore, the deceased parent may have previously played a significant role in caring for the surviving parent. This task is now likely to fall to one of their adult children.[3] Generally, parent–adult child relationships are characterized by mutual support and obligation, but the death of a parent is a defining moment in the relationship with the parent left behind, a moment when the balance of support between parent and adult child is most likely to change.

The surviving parent may be emotionally despondent or depressed, lonely, isolated, or even ill. After losing a parent, adults often feel closer to the surviving parent and they may start to visit or at least talk with the surviving parent more often. However, increased contact, in and of itself, does not necessarily indicate closer or more positive involvement with the parent; this contact may occur out of obligation or desire.

ACCEPTANCE AND POSITIVE CHANGE

Positive change in intergenerational relationships sometimes occurs when an adult makes a greater effort in the relationship with the surviving parent. Such efforts may reflect a new emotional maturity and responsibility that is inspired by the parent's death and the surviving parent's needs.

Before Marsha's mother died of cancer, they talked at length about their lives and about death. Marsha describes her mother's death as a "beautiful" experience because of the way her mother handled her illness and death. Marsha emphasizes that her mother's desires played a role in improving the relationship with her father:

> My father and I had a very strained relationship for almost twenty-five years prior to my mother's illness. On the day she was told her illness was terminal, she asked me to talk to my father and get to know him. She told me that he was a good man, but he just cannot express his feelings. For her sake, I made a very strong effort to finally get to know him and what his life had been like. Even though I had lived with him for thirty-nine years, I had no idea of what he liked, what he had done, or how he had grown up. Getting to know my father has had a tremendous impact on helping me cope with my mother's death. I only wish we had been able to communicate forty years ago – it would have definitely shaped my life much differently.

Since her mother's death, Marsha feels closer to her father and believes that her father is less critical and demanding as well as more supportive and loving toward her. Marsha's new approach to dealing with her father characterizes other changes in her life, changes that she associates with finally growing up:

> It's a strange feeling, but for the first time, I feel adult. . . . The things I always planned to do later are now the things I

do. Mama is not here now to give approval or disapproval. So it's really up to me now to live my life.

Bill also feels that he has matured as a result of his mother's death. He never felt particularly close to his father, and he communicated with his father primarily through his mother. Now that his mother is gone, he is talking directly with his father for the first time:

> He was always hard to talk to anyway. I guess fathers and sons are like that. . . . He worked two jobs all his life. The fact that I went away to college just made the gap bigger – as far as really talking. . . . If I did call, he asked how I was doing . . . and then gave the phone back to Mama. The fact that he can't give the phone to Mama now means that I'm asking him a lot of questions. I want us to be able to really talk to each other. . . . Here I am in my forties and really I'm just now being able to talk to Daddy. I guess I was talking to Daddy through Mama a lot of times.

Bill is motivated to cultivate the relationship with his father for several reasons. Talking with his father is one way of staying close to his mother. Bill is also trying to be more like his mother, a religious, charitable person who strongly valued family. The personal changes in Bill are enhancing his marriage, his relationship with his father, and the example he sets for his nine-year-old son:

> I was just reading this book. . . . It made me think about really telling Daddy, "I love you" and stuff like that. It was easy for me to tell that to Mama. . . . When Daddy and I used to see each other, we'd smile and shake hands. Now,

when Daddy got off the airplane, I gave him a big hug. I hug my son, Trey, a lot. So I guess I'm trying to show Trey that even men can hug each other and there's nothing wrong with showing feeling toward another man.

The surviving parent may also change in ways that make it easier for the bereaved adult to become more accepting and supportive of the parent. For instance, the parent may have always been very difficult, but may be less so following the loss of his or her spouse. Positive change in the intergenerational relationship is most likely when the child is responsive to changes in the parent and is motivated to make the relationship better.

Bobby, forty-one, always felt closer to his father than his mother, but even the relationship with his father was somewhat distant. One of the best qualities of that relationship was his father's willingness to protect Bobby from his mother:

> He was an interface with my mother, who I don't get along with very well. It was always like, "Well, Dad, Mother's acting crazy." He was kind of a buffer.... There's always been some problem with mom. In any family, there's a problem person and she's the problem person.

Bobby was very concerned that the relationship with his mother would only worsen after his father's death, and he is surprised to find that the relationship is actually improving. He attributes much of the change to his mother:

> I lost the interface with my mother, and our relationship has gotten better and closer. It's like we both realize that we have to get along. She's been remarkably

better behaved. . . . She's not as volatile . . . not as verbally inappropriate. She would even, when she realizes that she has gone too far, she would apologize.

It is no coincidence that Bobby is coming to terms with this relationship after his father's death. This death has forced Bobby to think of himself as an adult with responsibilities to his family. Bobby attributes some of the change in this relationship to his own changing attitudes:

I keep wishing she could be like Beaver Cleaver's mother but it's not going to happen. So it's coming to terms with how she is and just kind of accepting her – who she is – and accepting the relationship for what it is.

Bobby is pleased that the relationship is better, but he is not confident about the future. His mother's health is in decline and her memory seems to be deteriorating. He feels certain that he will eventually have to provide more care for his mother, and he knows that "being a long-term caregiver can be a wearing thing."

Bobby is trying to come to terms with the difficult lifelong relationship with his mother even as this relationship continues to change. How well he is able to negotiate these terms will determine how his mother's eventual death will affect him.

Like Bobby, some adults make more of an effort to understand and cope with their difficult parent. Underlying this attempt at understanding and tolerance may be a desire to be a different kind of person. Many stories of personal change include some conscious effort to be more accepting and supportive of the surviving parent. This effort will almost certainly provide some solace to the bereaved adult when their surviving parent dies.

Intergenerational relationships also can improve after the dying parent asks the child to make a greater effort with the surviving parent. Throughout life, Lois's relationship with her father was strained and painful, but Lois and her father shared personal thoughts and feelings in the last two weeks of his life. He told Lois that he was proud of her and he apologized for all the pain he had caused. He talked to Lois about dying and she was transformed by this experience. She can "almost forgive" her father for her difficult childhood and now feels that she had a special relationship with her father, based on those last two weeks. Lois also has a new appreciation for her father's relationship with her mother:

> I found out since he died that he kept my mother at her best because since he's died, she's just out of control. . . . I didn't realize how much he tolerated. . . . He said, "You have to promise me a couple of things." He said, "I love your mother to pieces but don't ever let her live with you. . . . God, Lois, she's like hell to live with." . . . Now I realize how she really is.

Incredible personal change characterizes Lois's life. After her father's death, she quit a high-powered job and night classes to spend more time with her family. She completely altered her priorities and she is now most focused on her son and husband. She also feels that her relationship with her mother has changed:

> I tolerate her a little more because I know she's lonely. And Dad told me not to pick on her too bad. He did. He told me, "You know, Lois, she's not easy to live with, get along with, but please try not to pick on her." It's like, okay, so I'm trying.

Lois was never close to her father in life. But in death, she feels a special bond with him. She attempts to carry out his wish of tolerating her mother. On the other hand, his newfound influence leaves Lois with a revised vision of her mother: as more difficult than Lois ever knew. Lois is motivated to believe in this "revision" of her mother because it is compatible with the version of her father as a loving and proud father. To resolve the troubled past with her father, Lois must now believe that her mother is a difficult person. Of course, this may make it even more difficult to resolve the eventual loss of her mother.

DEMANDS AND STRAINS

Adults are much more likely to report positive change than negative change in the relationship with their surviving parent. Yet, of course, some adult children do experience more strain and conflict with a parent following the loss. The surviving parent's involvement in new intimate relationships and long-term problems between the generations can each contribute to strain in relationships with surviving parents.

Romance

Although both men and women experience distress because they miss their partner, widowed men and women typically face different sorts of stress in their new widowed status.[4] On average, women experience more financial strain following widowhood, whereas men tend to experience more social isolation, loneliness, and the absence of any close confiding relationship. Women are more likely than men to have close, confiding relationships

outside of marriage, with friends, adult children, and other relatives. In turn, widowed men may be more likely than widowed
women to seek a new partner to assuage their feelings of loneliness and isolation. In fact, widowed men are much more likely
than widowed women to begin new relationships and to remarry.[5]
But what happens to intergenerational relationships when parents
find romance?

About a quarter of the bereaved adults whom I spoke with have
a surviving parent who started dating after the death. Since almost
all of the parents involved in new relationships were fathers, my
discussion pertains primarily to how adults feel about their father's
dating. Most of these adults generally approve of their parent's
involvement in a new relationship. In fact, they are often happy
for their parent and pleased that the parent has someone to care
for him or her. Marilyn describes how she felt about her father's
remarriage to her mother's sister following her mother's death:

> This is a wonderful, wonderful woman. And she had never
> married. . . . She took care of everybody and was having a
> real hard time financially. And Daddy was lonely. . . . It
> was wonderful. . . . He told me that that was one of the
> best things he ever did. He was happy.

On the other hand, some dating situations can create strain
and conflict. In particular, situations in which the child feels
that the parent is disrespectful of the deceased parent are con-
ducive to fractured intergenerational ties. In almost all cases, perceptions of disrespect are colored by the adult's past with both
parents.

Ella's mother died of complications associated with diabetes.
Ella's father was an alcoholic until Ella, now thirty-six, was eight,

and until that time, Ella helped her mother take care of and cover for her father. As Ella grew older, she increasingly blamed her mother for her father's alcoholism:

> My mother was very overweight. She was like three hundred pounds at probably her peak. She was very large and she didn't take much care of how she looked. She didn't care if she didn't take a bath every day. . . . She didn't wear makeup very much and I thought, "Well, mother, if you looked better then maybe Daddy would be better. . . . You could at least get up and get dressed or you could comb your hair." . . . I'm sure she didn't feel like it. But to her that wasn't important and she would get upset with me. I can't go out of the house without my makeup on or my hair fixed or whatever. I guess I've gone to the opposite extreme from her. . . . People liked her for who she was and it didn't matter. She was that secure. . . . I don't know. Maybe I resented that because I was always so insecure.

After her mother died, Ella felt a great deal of regret about the way she treated her mother earlier in life, and about blaming her mother for her father's alcoholism. She began to understand more about why she had always been so harsh with her mother:

> I did have a lot of resentment for my mother . . . because I was really upset with Daddy for not being there for me when I was younger. . . . I was able to . . . apologize for that, at least get it out just before she died so that I didn't have to carry that guilt around but I'm sorry that I didn't learn that earlier so that we could've had resentment-free time while she was alive.

But Ella did not manage to completely resolve all the old issues before her mother's death. In response, Ella is changing to
become more like her mother. Ella, who always saw her presentation of self as opposite to that of her overweight mother, has
gained twenty pounds since her mother died. The lack of resolution is also evident in a changing relationship with her father.
While her mother was alive, Ella often treated her with disdain
and disrespect. She now sees her mother in a new light and she
appreciates her mother's good qualities. Her father, on the other
hand, is seeing someone new and Ella is furious at what she views
as a lack of respect for her mother:

> There's a big rift with me and my dad. . . . I think it's dis-
> respectful for him to be seeing someone so soon. . . . What
> is it? Three months? They started seeing each other very
> regularly. . . . He's doing things that none of us could ever
> get him to do with us, like going to college football
> games. . . . One of my friends came for dinner. . . . My fa-
> ther talked, constantly, the whole time. I never heard him
> make small talk before and it's like he is changing because
> my mother was such an extrovert that he didn't have
> a chance to say anything before. . . . He's joining groups
> now. . . . I just don't like the dating part. . . . I didn't think
> he was acting the way a widower should act. . . . I'm just
> resentful right now with him. My mother saw him through
> the times that he drank and didn't leave him. . . . I feel, in
> a way, like he's leaving her.

Ella feels angry with her father for finally leaving her mother.
But Ella may be even more upset with herself because she regrets
that she abandoned her mother while her mother was living. In

an effort to resolve past issues with her mother, Ella is now her mother's defender.

Jeannie also feels that her father is treating a new partner better than he ever treated her mother. Again, it is not dating per se that troubles Jeannie; it is the perception that her surviving parent mistreated her lost parent. Jeannie always felt that she could talk to her mother about anything. Her mother's death due to cancer left Jeannie feeling depressed and lonely. Jeannie's relationship with her father only contributes to her sense of isolation.

Jeannie and her father were never emotionally close, but they bonded in caring for her mother in the months before her death. As her mother's health deteriorated, Jeannie and her father provided all of the home care for her mother. Jeannie says, "I felt like my dad and I were doing it alone. It was us against the world." Jeannie and her father share a sense of loss for her mother, but they are coping with the loss in different ways. Jeannie does not want to let go of the feelings of loss. She has abandoned friends who do not want to discuss her mother's death. Her father, on the other hand, is getting on with life in dramatic fashion. He is dating someone new and seems to Jeannie like a changed person. Jeannie is upset with him, in part because he never treated her mother as well as he treats his new romantic partner:

> I didn't mind at first that he was dating someone.... On the other hand, I feel that he hasn't spent his time griev-ing.... He talks to me a little differently than before – like he told me not to drop by on Sundays.... He is so active and busy now. Why didn't he do that when he and my mom were married? It would have made their marriage a lot better than him just sitting around not doing any-thing.... He is a new person and it bugs me now because

I think why didn't he do that with Mom? He does all this stuff for this new lady.

On some level, Jeannie wonders whether her father did nothing before "because Mom made him that way." But issues of abandonment abound in Jeannie's experience. She cannot relent in the condemnation of her father because it would mean that she has abandoned her mother just as her father has. In addition, Jeannie feels that her father has abandoned *her*. In a sense, she feels the loss of both parents.

Long-Term Problems

Although the death of a parent sometimes leads to positive change in long-difficult relationships with surviving parents, long-term problems in relationships with one parent often become more salient and disturbing in the wake of the other parent's death.

Rhoda's relationship with her mother has always been strained. She always viewed her mother as largely responsible for her parents' volatile marriage. Rhoda's mother was critical of her father while he was living and remains critical of him even now, one year after his death:

Mom would scold him because his oxygen tank would make marks on the floor. . . . He would call me when mom wasn't around. He thought she'd criticize what he was saying. I think there were times when he used to go to a pay phone if he wanted to talk. . . . After the death it was difficult because Mom was so angry. She was going through a very angry time. She couldn't find silly little things like the battery charger for her VCR. She just knew Dad put it somewhere. She was making a list that she was going to tell him about whenever she saw him again.... He left ashes in the fireplace. He was supposed to clean that.

Rhoda's relationship with her mother suffers, in part, because her father no longer serves as a buffer between her and her mother. In addition, Rhoda's mother interferes with Rhoda's expression of her own loss and sadness:

> In a sense there was anger at her for not letting me grieve.... Dad had to listen to the griping all the time and now I hear it. She still was very critical about people, even about the flowers she got.... I didn't see a change in her and I wanted to. I think I wanted to see her as more human and that didn't come out.... I had a lot of anger toward her.

When marital strife between parents is high before one of them dies, the emotions of the surviving parent and adult child can collide. A sense of shared loss is absent, and the adult who experiences the loss in this lonelier context may be defensive and protective of the deceased parent. This social and psychological context makes it more difficult for the child to cope with and recover from the loss. The surviving parent's continuing animosity toward the deceased parent can drive a deeper wedge between the surviving parent and adult child.

Helen, fifty-two, describes how the decade-old divorce of her parents interfered with her relationship with her surviving mother:

> It's been hard for my mother because she really kept a lot of animosity.... She was just really, really angry about it

all. This is the hard thing: No one in the family can feel like I feel about him.

Helen, like many adults, suddenly and strongly identified with her father following his death. She is struck by how much she now sees her father in herself: "The things I care about, the basics of my life . . . I learned from him. Not my mother." Strongly identifying with her father keeps her father alive for her and comforts her at the same time. On the other hand, identifying with her father means more fully divorcing herself from her mother, just as her father did. Allegiance to the deceased parent often means fighting or abandoning the surviving parent.

The death of one parent can lead adults to reevaluate the relationship with their surviving parent. This provides an opportunity for improving the relationship. On the other hand, it is striking that many adults seem to have no increased awareness that the second parent will inevitably die. Some individuals are quite bereft over the loss of one parent, perhaps even regretting that they had not handled the relationship differently while the parent was alive. Yet it seems to be difficult for adults to realize that the second parent will ultimately die and that they will have another set of unresolved issues to deal with. For example, Rhoda's relationship with her difficult mother seems to have been unaffected by the experience of her father's death: "It was hard for me to go back over there again to see my mother. . . . She's a woman of steel. Nothing will ever happen to her. . . . I mean she's the terminator."

Long-term problems between the parents can produce a parent's insensitivity to the child's pain and loss. In these instances, distance and perhaps even hostility between the parents mean that, although the adult child may be experiencing the loss of a loved and valued person, the surviving parent does not share the loss. When a child is grieving for a lost parent, having to cope with a surviving parent who does not share the sense of loss and perhaps even continues to criticize and complain about the deceased spouse strongly serves to alienate the adult child from the surviving parent.

The parent's insensitivity to the loss also makes it harder for the child to cope with his or her own grief. Jonathon's parents never divorced, but he describes his father as helpless and overly dependent and demanding where his mother was concerned:

> My mother waited on him hand and foot.... Last May when I talked to my mother ... I said, get out of there even if it's just for three days so you can break what appeared to us to be an unhealthy relationship.... She said no, she was going to stick it through. They had an old-fashioned marriage, very loyal. And so she did stick it through.

His father's long-term dependence on his mother bothered Jonathon a great deal. His father shifted this dependence onto his adult children after the loss. Jonathon identifies strongly with his mother since her death, and his father's new dependence gives Jonathon the opportunity to break away from his father. On some level, Jonathon does this for his mother:

> My father was so self-centered that the time that we were at home we were more concerned about his welfare and never even got the chance to have this communal, family time of grieving together.... I feel that he usurped our natural right to that experience. So that's part of my resentment.... There wasn't any support from my father in

terms of sympathy for what grief I might have about the loss of my mother. . . . The anger that I felt toward him . . . has permanently soured my relationship with my father.

Role Reversal

Perhaps the greatest change in relationships with surviving parents centers around dependency and caregiving. Most adults begin to worry about their surviving parent more and to feel that their parent has become more emotionally dependent. In turn, the bereaved may find that he or she spends more time caring for the parent than before the loss. Such care does not necessarily involve intensive caregiving to a dependent parent but, more often, is simply a greater involvement with and monitoring of the parent's needs. These changes arise from the adult child's concern over the parent's grief and because the period following one parent's death is a likely time for role reversal to begin or to accelerate.

The surviving parent may grieve intensely over the loss of his or her spouse, and witnessing this grief can be painful for adults. Ginger feels that her parents had a good marriage and finds that her mother's loss is the most challenging aspect of coping with her father's death:

> I feel, as an adult child, that I'm starting . . . to move into the parent/child swap and feeling like I should be taking care of my mother. And this is something I could not help her with and that hurt a lot.

Positive personal changes in Ginger make it easier for her to help her mother, but the role reversal commonly experienced following one parent's death can be a source of considerable strain for adults who are not coping as well as Ginger.

Most people find that caring for an aging parent is stressful, especially when the parent is mentally or physically impaired. Caring for a parent is also difficult when the relationship was strained or difficult earlier in life. Jonathon finds it difficult to care for his father, in part because they were never close:

> My father and I had a terrible relationship before my mother's death. Afterward, my dad was so overwhelmed that I had to put aside my feelings and help him. . . . He was such a jerk that everyone else pretty much just stays away from him. . . . My father . . . has been unable to cope with life and shows no interest in the things that my mother would have cherished – her family, her grandkids, her friends. My dad says he should have been the one to die and there is no way to argue with that statement.

Even when the past relationship with the parent was close, caregiving can be stressful. Responsibility for a parent's well-being often interferes with the adult's other roles, relationships, and responsibilities or at least adds to the cumulative set of duties that the bereaved adult must juggle.

Out of concern for the parent, many adults begin to play a greater role in monitoring the parent's well-being, even in the absence of hands-on caregiving. This sets the stage for role reversal, as the child begins to parent the parent more than the child is parented. Ginger explains:

> I am more nurturing of her. I am more protective than I ever was before. . . . I call her a lot more frequently to check

in and make sure that she's okay. I feel more the parent now than ever before.

Although role reversal occurs in many parent/adult child relationships, some adults feel more emotionally dependent on the surviving parent than they were prior to the loss. Many of the adults I spoke with told me that they need their parent now more than they did prior to the loss. This increased dependence can be tied to a need to replace the emotional reliance on the lost parent as well as the growing recognition that the adult child will eventually be an orphaned adult. Of course, an adult's feeling of greater need does not preclude increased dependence of the parent on the child.

CONCLUSION

The death of a parent is an important developmental milestone for many adults, and it often leads to a review of the relationship with the surviving parent. The death of a parent also marks a turning point in many intergenerational relationships. It is a likely time to begin to experience role reversal with a parent, and this contributes to the transformation of adult identity – to the sense of becoming an independent adult. In addition, the death of a parent leads to a restructuring of families in that a family figure, sometimes a very central figure, is no longer present and other family members must renegotiate that social and psychological space. In contrast to marital relationships, intergenerational relationships tend to reach a new balance that is more positive than negative for most families. This can occur even when adults must assume new responsibilities in caring for the surviving parent.

Change in the self can also drive change in intergenerational ties. For those individuals who feel a significant shift in maturity and responsibility for others following a parent's death, intergenerational ties often improve. These adults are more likely to make an effort to accept their parent as is and perhaps attempt to resolve old issues before that parent dies. Adults with a difficult family history are more likely to have trouble with the surviving parent. This trouble may be especially likely to surface when the surviving parent is perceived as the cause of much past misery in the family and when the child modifies the relationship with him or her in order to resolve past problems with the deceased parent. These modifications sometimes contribute to increased conflict and bad feelings toward the surviving parent. Bereaved adults should be aware that new and growing tensions with the surviving parent will almost certainly complicate issues of resolution and recovery after the surviving parent dies. The past is never fully left behind. But the present may be modified in some effort to resolve the past.

8

MY BROTHER'S KEEPER

My brother, who is the oldest child, lived only seventy-five miles away from Mother....I lived 900 miles away....He could have provided more help and support to my mother during her last six months....I'm having a difficult time forgiving him for not being there more for my mother and sister.

NORA, AGE FIFTY-ONE

My sister has been a great deal of support for me since my mother's death....She is twelve years older than I am and we have always seen this age difference as something that has kept us from being closer. But now she has played a leader and mentor role. This has really made me feel very respectful towards her.

ANGIE, AGE TWENTY-NINE

The death of a parent can provide siblings with the opportunity to come closer together, to share their loss with others who uniquely understand the nature of the loss, and to provide and receive support that may ease the loss. On the other hand, the death of a parent is a stressful event: Property must be settled and dispersed and old sibling rivalries and inequities may resurface.

Questions about sibling relationships elicited some of the most lengthy and emotional responses in my interviews with bereaved adults. One of the clearest themes in these interviews is that one cannot generalize about relationships among siblings, even in the same family. Rather, the relationship of each sibling with another is unique. It is not at all unusual for adults to report a close and confiding relationship with one sibling and a conflict-ridden and distant relationship with another. Moreover, each child in the family had a unique relationship with the lost parent. In this sense, each sibling experiences a different kind of loss.

CLOSENESS

Siblings are especially important sources of support for adults who lose a parent. Many of the adults I interviewed say that they feel closer to at least one of their siblings than they did prior to the loss. Angie, a twenty-nine-year-old woman, describes how her sister served in this role, "My sister has been great. She listens without reproach. She understands without my explaining. She doesn't judge my views."

A sense of shared grief and loss often occurs in relationships with family members, especially siblings, who knew and loved the unique person who died. A sense of shared loss facilitates empathy; it helps siblings to understand the depth of one another's pain. Marta, forty, explains how the loss of her father brought her closer to one of her brothers:

> One of my brothers is a Methodist preacher and he performed the funeral service. He had done so for other family members but this is the first time he had cried. It was very painful to watch him struggling to continue. I wanted to walk over, put my arm around him and say, "You don't have to do this, let's go home." It was a good experience

in that he said many things that my other brother and I wanted to express and it made me feel much closer to this brother.... While my father was dying and for a few days after, we had many good talks and grew much closer than we had been before.

Some bereaved adults link increased closeness with a sibling to the resolution of old family issues. Steven is from a Chinese American family with four sons. Steven emphasizes that the family style has always been one of stoicism, emotional distance, and respect. He describes how his wife and younger brother resolved an old conflict as a result of his father's illness and death:

My brother, Brian, and my wife had it out a few years ago. Somebody said something, somebody said something else, and it's, "Okay, fine, so we're apart." One thing my folks were continually fighting for was family unity: "You got to be together, you're strong. You're apart, you break." So Brian won't apologize and my wife won't apologize 'cause each of them thinks that they're right. But my dad forced the issue at the hospital and said, "You guys shake hands." So Brian and my wife shake hands and they're trying to make things better. And then after the funeral, my mom made us all sit in the living room. We stayed up until three o'clock to hash out anything we needed to hash out.... Now we have a common goal of trying to help our mom get things okay.

In some families, siblings have different ways of expressing grief, and this can cause conflict between siblings. Yet in Steven's family, the four sons all reacted in the same way. They carried out their assigned duties in settling the estate and they kept their emotions in check:

> All of my brothers were very composed.... 'Cause when we grew up, we didn't see very much emotion at home.... When my dad was on his death bed, he was saying, "Don't cry, be strong, stand on your feet," which is like, "suppress yourself, deny anything's happening."

The sons grew closer in their united front of emotional stability and in the teamwork required to settle their father's estate. This was particularly important in Steven's family because his mother was so outwardly distraught and emotional following the loss. The sons worked together to protect their mother, take care of their father's business, and provide financial security for their mother. They assumed many of the roles previously held by their emotionally distant father. In this sense, their increased closeness was not so much emotional as it was practical, yet it served to console each of them. The shifts in Steven's sense of self and in his family carry forward their family culture and tradition.

Diana, forty-two, and her sister also resolved some family differences as a result of their father's illness and death. Diana was only twenty when her mother died. Her father remarried just five years before his death and Diana never felt close to her stepmother. Diana describes how she finally grew closer to her sister in a face-off with their stepmother while their father was ill:

> The funny thing out of all that whole mess is that my sister and I never got along very well. But now it's like we talk five times a day.... We sort of feel like we're all we have now so I'm real close to her. She has a three-year-old

and we all went to Boston and Maine this summer. You know, a family trip. That's just real funny.... My friends just laugh. They can't believe it.... A lot of it was there were some bad hospital scenes with my stepmother and I rallied to my sister's side.... You know, there's this sense of family or something.

A new sense of family and the importance of siblings to maintaining family are common responses to a parent's death. The reported increase in sibling closeness does not appear to be temporary in most cases. For instance, Diana's closer relationship to her sister had been in place for three years at the time of our interview.

Some siblings become closer when an adult child suddenly reclaims a previously abandoned family following a parent's death. This usually occurs in families where an estranged child had a difficult relationship with the parent. In such cases, new sibling ties may be quite close. For instance, Stephanie and her brother grew up with an unpredictable and unreliable mother. The children were often left on their own as their mother pursued her latest love interest. Stephanie's response to her mother was to make every effort to get close to her. Her brother, Steve, chose a different strategy: He stayed away from his mother. After their mother died, Steve initiated contact with Stephanie:

My brother kind of lost touch with the family for a while.... But ever since my mom died, he's flipped a hundred and eighty degrees.... He calls me all the time.... We see each other all the time.... I called him and said, "I'm coming up this weekend." So he and his girlfriend are all excited and they're making plans.... In the past we weren't close at all. I guess in a way he just chose to not really be part of the family. . . . He was always real distant. . . . Now we talk on the phone a lot. He calls, which is really surprising for him. I mean we used to go months without ever hearing from him.

Stephanie's mother died almost a year ago. She and Steve remain close and she feels that they have a newly defined family. These are new roles for Stephanie and her brother – roles that help them to resolve their painful family history. These new family ties and roles have been good for both of them in that their "new family" is stable and centered without their unpredictable mother at its helm.

RESTRUCTURED FAMILY ROLES

Parents often play the role of bringing adult siblings together and serving as the communications and holiday center for the family. After parents die, siblings must renegotiate their roles within the family and many adults feel that the siblings now constitute the family. Greg, thirty-eight, now feels more responsible for maintaining family ties:

> I remember Mother saying that one day my sister and I would be all each other had left of our integral family and it is so true. I have come to appreciate what a fantastic person my sister has grown up to be.

Similarly, forty-one-year-old Joyce told me, "My siblings and I talk more because we don't have mom to keep us connected anymore."

In many families, one child will take on the parental role of making sure that all the siblings stay in touch, see one another, and know about family news. As a sibling assumes this new role as family leader, a new sense of responsibility and importance emerges in that sibling's sense of self. As a result, the other siblings have a new anchor to help reestablish the sense of family.

A newly structured family can emerge when one sibling assumes a parental role in relation to another sibling – a role that previously may have been filled by the parent. Although Diana does not feel closer to her brother, she sees that they have a different kind of relationship:

> My dad took a pretty active part in telling us kids what
> to do for the past twenty years since my mother died.
> I mean, he wasn't like a pest about it, but he was just
> interested. . . . My brother has taken on this daddy role in
> terms of offering advice.

Terri, thirty-four, was drafted into her mother's role with her sisters. Terri always viewed her mother as a sounding board, a source of advice, and a person with whom she could share her accomplishments and concerns. Terri's sisters also relied on their mother, although in a different way. Terri describes how her two sisters tried to pull her into the mediator role that her mother used to play:

> My mom . . . must have, over the years, kind of run inter-
> ference between my two older sisters and I never knew
> it. . . . I think she kind of buffered that and acted as the
> mediator. As Mother became more and more ill, I began
> getting phone calls from my sisters. Jan calling and saying,

"You will never believe what Tricia has done." And I was so frustrated. An hour later the phone would ring and sister Tricia would call and say, "I think I'm going to kill Jan. I have just had it with her." And so what happened was, they began, I believe without realizing it, but they began to put me in that role of kind of running in between them and trying to make everybody happy. That was real hard. . . . I've had to work hard to set my boundaries. . . . I love both of them and they're my family now. I don't want to alienate either one of them.

As Terri's mother grew sicker with cancer, Terri had to adjust to a changing relationship with her: Terri asked for less and offered more. Although this was a loss for Terri, she managed to make the necessary adjustments. The demands of her sisters provided additional stress for Terri, and she developed new roles in the family — some variation on the roles previously filled by her mother. The sibling family experiences shifts that are sometimes difficult as it achieves a modified version of the old family.

Restructuring also occurs when adult children find an opportunity to receive *less* parenting from their siblings. Some adults are viewed, for the first time, as adults. This gives them new status and new roles in the family. Connie, twenty-nine, explains, "Helping my siblings cope during the last weeks of my mother's illness and after her death has finally caused them to see me as an adult."

Similarly, Jackie's seven siblings were particularly worried about her when her father died because Jackie, thirty-six, had been extraordinarily close to her father and because the siblings had always viewed Jackie as the baby of the family. The children's mother died when Jackie was only ten and their father raised Jackie "single-handedly." Jackie now feels closer to all of her siblings and also feels that her relationship to them has changed greatly because they no longer view her as the baby of the family:

> Since I'm the youngest, I have historically done as the older siblings suggested. . . . After the funeral, the younger siblings made more of the decisions than ever before. . . . My relationships with my oldest two siblings is the most dramatically different. In the past they acted as surrogate parents but now I'm a free agent. I don't let them tell me what to do anymore and I don't model myself after them.

Jackie's family of siblings has been modified as a result of their father's death. Concomitantly, Jackie's sense of self has changed:

> I feel like . . . I have to be a complete adult now. I try to draw on the strengths of my parents. . . . I have a fuller sense of who I am. I have a stronger self-definition of myself as a chip off the old block. . . . The loss makes you more compassionate toward others. You understand what grief is all about – what others might be going through. You become more parental toward others.

CONFLICT AND STRAIN

Although some siblings become closer following a parent's death, other sibling relationships suffer. Discordant grief experiences and disagreement over the details of dealing with the death contribute to difficulties in sibling relationships.

Discordant Grief

In every family, each child knows the parent in a different way, and, as a result, each sibling experiences a different kind of loss when the parent dies. Helen describes the distinctly different father that each of her siblings knew:

> My siblings weren't as close to my father.... Each one of us knew a different father. We knew him when he was younger and older, at different times in his life...so we all knew something different. As a girl, I'm sure that I knew him in a different way.... After the death I was talking about all the songs Dad used to sing. My half-brother was just totally stunned. He said, "Well, he couldn't sing. I never heard him sing," and I said, "Well, he sang all the time." Then all of a sudden it dawned on me...he knows something else about my father and we talked and shared stories. My younger brothers had different experiences with him too.... They had these fishing stories with my father.

Even when siblings have different views of a parent, the opportunity for shared grief exists. On the other hand, in addition to feeling a different kind of loss, each child may express feelings of loss in different ways. This discordance in expression of emotion may disturb a sibling who feels as though another sibling is over- or underreacting to the loss. Some people cope best by repressing their emotions or by focusing on the future rather than the present loss. Siblings who express their loss in different ways may become upset with one another. For example, one sibling may be openly expressive, while another sibling feels that extreme distress makes the loss more difficult for everyone. Alternatively, one sibling may view the absence of distress in another sibling as insensitivity. Discordant emotion often involves a gender component where sisters feel that brothers are uncaring and unfeeling.

Helen had a much more emotional reaction than her brothers when their father died. She describes her loss: "My father loved me more than anyone in this life, that's what I've lost." She became very upset with her brothers for their seeming lack of emotion:

> We started to quarrel about my father's care. The main thing was my brothers kind of threw their force shields up and I was the one hurting.... That made it difficult for them.... They never broke down and cried. I remember thinking, "What's the matter with them?" And I'm sure that they said, "What's the matter with you?" It seems to me that they were just so rational about everything. They drove me crazy.... At the funeral, my brothers were dry-eyed. I thought, "How can they?... This is tearing me apart."... I was really surprised that they did not show the grief that I felt.... We haven't really gotten back on good ground yet.

Different experiences as well as individual temperaments and personality may lead each child to a different view of the parent. These different views of the same parent may reflect individual perceptions, but they may also reflect reality. Parents often treat their children in distinct ways. Abusive parents may single out only one child for abuse even in very large families, and many children are able to identify a parent's favorite child.[1]

Tina has one brother and one sister. Their childhood was characterized by tension and unpredictability: They never knew when their father might have a violent outburst. Tina explains that all of them had different relationships with their parents and that she was the most likely target of her father's anger and violence:

> My brother didn't get it because he was a boy. My sister didn't get it because she was a little deaf girl in her father's eyes. But there I was – reflecting a lot of stuff back to him because he could see himself in me a lot of the time and he could see my mother in me. I challenged him on his behavior – when I wasn't afraid of him.

Tina and her sister shouldered the burden of caring for her parents when they were ill, and they now shoulder the burden of closing down their parent's home and settling their estate. Tina is angry with her brother for not doing his share. She is also angry with him because he and Tina express their loss in very different ways:

> It's hard because my brother and I were very close.... He was my big brother. I'm the baby of the family. I'm not supposed to have all this responsibility. That's what I've always been told. I guess I expected a little bit more from him.... I thought it was going to be different after Mom and Dad both died. I had felt ... that we would depend on each other a lot, but it just got too hard for him to be here and to be going through their stuff.... He just kind of shut it off. He quit coming up here for several months.... That was another kind of loss. After my parents died my brother didn't want me to cry because that was hard for him. I was on the phone and just sobbing and he was saying, "Just stop it, stop it. I need you to stop." It was extremely difficult.

Tina used to feel close to her brother, but since her parents died, she feels estranged from him:

> I know that he loved them and cared about them . . . but he just couldn't be around it. He should have been with me at the hospital. . . . I understand how he is but to be honest with myself, I'm real resentful that he couldn't grow up and deal with it.

Tina has always held a position of responsibility and maturity in her family. She and her mother were victims of her father's violent temper. During Tina's childhood, she did her best to support and care for her mother and for her older sister who was deaf; Tina adds, "Before it really would have been appropriate, my mother and I were best friends; she relied on me for support before I was even an adult."

Tina now assumes the identity of family matriarch. She cared for her parents who were ill and now she alone is handling the resolution of her parents' estate, which is characterized by debt and complexity. She worries over the well-being of her siblings and makes sure that the siblings stay in touch with one another.

In many families, one sibling has special needs or problems apart from the parent's death. These problems, combined with the parent's death, can evoke concern and worry in other siblings. Even though a stronger sibling may care for the needy sibling and perhaps even offer assistance voluntarily, the worry and concern is often stressful for the stronger sibling. Again, a gender component is apparent where a sister is much more likely to express concern about a brother. Marta, forty, worries a lot about one of her brothers: "My younger brother is depression-prone and this year, he has lost his father, and his marriage ended. I worry even more about him than I did before our father's death."

Casey is extremely worried about her four brothers – all of them unexpressive and stoic, much like their recently deceased father. Casey's unique life history led to unusually tight-knit relationships among her siblings, especially in childhood. Her mother died when Casey, the oldest of the children, was six. Casey's father, a farmer, felt strongly about raising his young children, even though several relatives pressured him to separate the children and send them to other relatives. But Casey's father was clearly overwhelmed by the task of parenting his young charges. As a result, the children became heavily reliant on one another:

> My dad was very quiet and his way of dealing with anything was to run off by himself, which made us kids mad. A lot of times we would be home by ourselves and he was off playing dominoes with his friends or doing something. He couldn't stand to be at home so he would go off. . . . So a lot of the time that we spent together was just us kids. . . . The way he handled things was really distant. But, at the same time, from the very beginning, he was determined to keep us all together.

Even into adulthood, the children stayed closely involved with one another and with their father. The two daughters eventually married – against their father's wishes. But the three sons stayed on with the father. At the time of his death, the sons were forty-one, forty-three, and forty-five years old. Casey is worried about how "the boys" will make it without their father:

> We're all so different in our ways of doing things. . . . I'm really concerned about them because I do a lot of the

talking. . . . The boys don't believe in talking about anything. So it kind of worries me that they have this one
focus in life and that focus was to take care of Daddy and
do what Daddy wanted. Now we don't have that focus
anymore.

Through her father's illness and even now as the children
deal with the loss of their father, the brothers' lack of emotion
and communication is difficult for Casey:

It was just really hard that they chose not to be with us at
the hospital. For them the way to handle anything is to
just ignore it and it'll be okay. . . . I'm really worried about
them. . . . My dad taught those boys how not to recognize
emotions.

Childhood circumstances bind Casey and her siblings together
to an extreme degree, even in adulthood. And these siblings remain united even beyond the death of their father and their own
individual differences. Casey's father left 600 acres of land to his
children. None of the children are financially well off, and selling
this land would make life easier for each of them. But the children
have made a joint decision to keep the family land together:

My dad was the magnet. He just kind of kept us in a circle –
in orbit around him. So now, that's not really there. I can't
find it. But I think there's little trails. We said all along,
we'd try to keep the land.

In part, keeping the land means keeping the brothers together under one roof. But the family unit is symbolic to them as well: Keeping the family home means keeping the family intact. Keeping

the family intact is a legacy handed down from Casey's father to his children. Perpetuating this legacy is a way to honor and respect their father

In Casey's family, all six children saw their father in the same light: They respected him and now feel a bit unmoored by his death. They share a sense of loss. In other families, the siblings do not agree on what was lost with the death of a parent. When views of a parent contrast greatly, especially when one sibling views the parent positively while another views the parent with disdain, siblings may clash following the loss. This happened in Joan's family.

Both of Joan's parents died within a week: Her mother had a heart attack and her father died a few days later following a stroke. Family is very important to Joan and she is close to five of her siblings, but she is upset with one brother who she feels mistreated her parents:

> My mom was always the peacemaker in the family. One of my brothers brought his children over for Mom to babysit. He always took advantage of her and never paid her. Mom and Dad were retired and only had small Social Security checks. About one week before they died, my Dad and brother had an argument over payment for babysitting. . . . This upset my Mom because my brother always threatened to not bring the kids back ever again. I feel my brother's argument had a lot to do with Mom having a heart attack. She loved her children and grandchildren — each and every one of them. It would have broken her heart if she never got to see them again. It was very unfair of him to do that. This has caused a lot of hard feelings.

Similarly, Clara believes that the major factor that makes it more difficult to cope with the loss of her mother is a brother who did not treat her mother very well:

An older brother had been very distant and unloving to Mom when she was alive.... This caused Mom a lot of pain.... His spouse really had been worse than he was.... I didn't appreciate how they treated Mother.... I have written them off for a meaningful relationship.

Clara and her brother are now completely estranged because she cannot forgive him for mistreating their mother. Ironically, Clara believes that the one positive thing resulting from her mother's death stems from the problems with her brother: "I have found more acceptance of my power and my abilities due to standing up to my brother's adverse behavior."

Disagreement over Details

Conflict between siblings may arise over funeral arrangements, expressions of grief, old rivalries, perceived mistreatment of the parent in the past, and innumerable other issues. One of the most likely points of conflict following a parent's death concerns the distribution of the parent's property and possessions. These disputes are not over mere material possessions; rather, they occur because the parent's possessions are symbolic of the parent.

Mary, fifty, views herself as the "classic middle child." She describes her four siblings as happily married, well educated, and financially well off, and she describes herself as low-income, divorced, and having a poor self-concept. Mary feels that she sacrificed much of her independence and autonomy to take care of her elderly parents, who were critical of Mary throughout life, even after they moved in with her. Mary never had a close relationship with her siblings, but she feels more distant from them since her parents have died. She attributes much of this distance to her siblings' insensitivity to Mary's need to keep more of her mother's possessions:

> When my parents moved in, I got rid of some of my furniture and my things so we could put out their things. Some of it was my stuff and some of it was their stuff. . . . I know it's not reasonable. I know that [my brothers and sisters] have a right to these things, so I know it's really kind of silly for me to be jealous over what they got. I guess I just wanted everything. . . . They want me to come up for Thanksgiving. . . . I don't want to see my mother's things.

Mary felt that her parent's possessions had, in a sense, become hers because both she and her parents relied on them. She is hurt that her siblings have less need for these items than she does, yet they want them anyway. She does not recognize that her parent's possessions may also have symbolic value for her siblings.

Patricia, thirty-two, also envies her three siblings, all of whom are married and have children. Patricia feels that she lost her family when her parents died, in part because her parents constituted family for Patricia but also because she has lost her family of siblings. Patricia and her siblings have argued frequently over her parent's possessions:

> My siblings turned on each other and I was made the biggest scapegoat. My two sisters ostracized me and withheld heirlooms, mementos, and even my own possessions that my father had been storing for me. The pain of simply

not having things that belonged to my parents has been startlingly intense, all the more because these things were denied me by siblings behaving viciously.... They have not responded to my efforts to contact them in a year.

A parent's possessions take on greater importance after he or she dies. They are not merely "things"; they are worldly symbols of the parent. Staying close to these special objects enables the mourning child to maintain a connection to the deceased parent. Jackie describes how her father's possessions console her in her time of loss:

Keeping some of his things, sometimes even using them – his coffee mug – or wearing them – his Army dog tag or a shirt – make it easier for me to cope. I constantly am drawn to situations, stories, clothing, and other things that remind me of him. Focusing on him in a positive way makes me feel better, like he is still around.

CHILDREN WHO CARE FOR IMPAIRED PARENTS

Gerontologists find that providing care to a widowed parent typically falls to one sibling in a family, usually a daughter.[2] The stress of this caregiving might be expected to cause sibling conflict. However, this is not a dominant theme in my interviews with bereaved adults. It may be that, after a parent dies, caregiving provided prior to the death seems much less salient than the death itself.[3] Those who provided care to their parent actually report better sibling relationships following the death than do those who did not provide care. Caregivers are more likely to report that a sibling helped to ease the loss and that they have been in more frequent contact with siblings since the death of the parent. Caregivers also report fewer sibling problems generally and fewer sibling problems around issues related to the loss. It may be that siblings appreciate the role served by a sibling who provided direct care to a parent, and the siblings then respond in a positive way to him or her.

Rhoda, forty-nine, is grateful to her younger sister, who now cares for her mother, following their father's death:

> I have felt a lot of guilt because Beverly was about an hour and a half from Mom so she has had the burden of taking care of the business and things, just all kinds of things. . . . I hope I have helped her. . . . I try to thank her a whole lot for being there.

Care providers may also come from families that place more emphasis on family responsibilities and cohesiveness. Terri was the primary caregiver to her mother for several years. Her two older sisters provided much less care, but Terri appreciates the role they played in helping their mother:

> I do feel really thankful and very proud of the way we all hung together because lots of decisions had to be made as far as my mother's care. . . . There was a lot of cooperation that the three of us had to do in order to carry out [my mother's] wishes. And I'm really thankful that we were able to set aside our own personal feelings at times about things in order to attain the end of her being happy – doing what made my mom happy.

The men and women I spoke with emphasized the difficulties of caring for an impaired parent, but they were almost unanimously pleased that they cared for the parent in his or her final days. Sharon is now comforted by the role she played in caring for her mother after she was diagnosed with cancer, nine months prior to her death. As Sharon's mother grew increasingly weak, it became clear that she would either have to be institutionalized or move in with Sharon. Sharon and her supportive husband invited Sharon's mother to move into their home:

> We took care of her. My parents did it for me for twenty years and I only did it for a month. It was very good. It was extremely important to us to let her spend her last days at home.

Tina, thirty-five, cared for both of her parents in the months leading to their deaths. Her mother died of cancer and her father died following a heart attack just three weeks later. She acknowledges the difficulties of caring for her parents, but is consoled by having provided that care:

> I don't have any regrets. I'm comforted in knowing that I did everything I could. I've said what I needed to say. I can't say that I would go back and change anything. I would still do just as much as I did.... I've told people I was very grateful to have the opportunity to care for my parents. They said, "Oh, it must have been just terrible for you and so disruptive to be doing all this." I said, "No, this allowed me and my children to spend time with my parents." This is something my brother and sister didn't have. They could have taken more part... but my sister has four kids and a full-time job. Understandably, she could not do that much to help. I think my brother... could not cope with

it. . . . He didn't want to cope with the fact that our parents were getting older and . . . that they were going to die.

Tina feels that caring for her parents helped her to recover from the death of her parents. She believes that her siblings are having more trouble dealing with the loss, in part because they were not involved in their parents' care:

I feel really sad for my sister and for my brother. My sister kept a lot of things in. She really wanted to spend more time with Dad or talk to him more, especially right after Mother died. But it was difficult for her – emotionally – to do it.

Providing care for a parent may help adults to recover from the loss with fewer feelings of regret.

CONCLUSION

Siblings play an important role in shaping an adult child's grief following parent loss. Overall, it appears that siblings are more likely to play a helpful role than an undermining role in helping adults to cope with a parent's death. Moreover, each child experiences the loss of a parent, but the practical and symbolic meaning of that loss differs for each child in the family. Sibling relationships are complex and also vary greatly in quality and dynamics, even within families. Within the same family, for instance, one sibling relationship may become closer while another may become more strained.

The family system is clearly altered by a parent's death, even when all of the children are adults. Families undergo psychological and social restructuring following the death. The nature of this restructuring depends on previous relationships within the family, the role previously filled by the deceased parent, current social contexts (e.g., contexts differ for men and women), and the history of the family. Adults often assume new roles in relation to one another following a parent's death, roles previously enacted by the deceased parent. The death of a parent liberates some adults to assume new roles in relation to siblings; for example, an adult who was always viewed as the baby of the family may become viewed as more mature and independent in relation to other family members. If the deceased parent played a central role in holding together a family characterized by strain and conflict, the death of that parent may free an adult child to leave the remaining family behind. On the other hand, some adult children come to play the role of the matriarch or patriarch of a family that has lost a central family figure. Many of these individuals feel that a torch has been handed to them to carry into the future.

9

RITE OF PASSAGE

I'm it...the main matriarchal figure! I feel a sudden sense of responsibility. MARINA, AGE FORTY-SEVEN

*My mother rarely treated me as an adult. Without her influ-
ence, I feel more grown-up and responsible for myself.*
ANGEL, AGE THIRTY-FIVE

The death of a parent is a wake-up call for most adults; it is
a call to confront the reality of mortality as the adult child
joins the next generation in line for death. In many ways, both
literal and symbolic, children remain children until their parents
die. Lynn explains:

> It makes you an orphan. I don't think it would make
> any difference how old you were. While your parents are
> living, every time you go back home, you become their
> child again and it's a parent-child relationship whether
> you're an adult or not. When you lose your parents,
> then you're the grown-up.... There's nobody to be a child
> with.

A sense of relinquishing childhood is a hallmark of parent loss. Thomas, thirty-six, describes the transition to adulthood:

> With her death it was a closure to my childhood. There was no way back, no path back to childhood. There's no reason for me to go back to Baltimore. The death gave me an opportunity to sit back and look at myself and say, "Okay, I'm truly an adult now. Now, am I self-sufficient?" Even though, you know . . . as long as your parent is alive you can always think, "Well, I can always go home." Well, home took on a different meaning to me now. Home is my house and my things.

THE PAST SHAPES THE FUTURE

The death of a parent is a turning point that can foster a new sense of responsibility for oneself and for others. This loss can create emotional upheaval that initiates an intense period of self-reflection and transformation. This upheaval can also cause depression, physical health problems, and alcohol problems. However, all adults are not affected in the same way by a parent's death. In fact, some adults actually experience an improvement in emotional well-being. An individual's emotional response depends on past and present social contexts, including childhood experiences with the parent, the quality of adult interactions with the parent, and the symbolic meaning of the loss. These contexts shape the direction in which the individual may change his or her adult identity and sense of self after the parent's death.

Adults are more likely to experience increased psychological distress following a mother's death than a father's death. Yet adults are more likely to increase their alcohol consumption following a father's death. These differences in response reflect long-term differences in children's relationships with mothers and fathers. Relationships with mothers tend to be emotionally closer than those with fathers, and mothers tend to be more emotionally expressive than fathers. The following passages from interviews with Alejandro and Sherry capture common differences in views of mothers and fathers. Alejandro, thirty-one, says of his father:

> When I was growing up, my relationship with my father . . . was not that close. It was a lot closer with my mother because my dad tended to be more of a disciplinarian. . . . He didn't show his emotions very much. . . . He showed his love by his actions. . . . He always thought that if he cried or laughed a lot in front of his children it was like a sign of weakness.

Sherry, also thirty-one, describes her relationship with her mother this way:

> I felt my mother loved me more than anybody does and it was, you know, unconditional love and she just accepted me and respected me. And we were best friends.

Yet relationships with mothers do not necessarily lead to a greater sense of loss than do relationships with fathers. Relationships with mothers tend to involve greater expression of feeling and emotion, while relationships with fathers tend to be based more on the sharing of activities than the sharing of emotion.[1] In turn, the loss of a mother may be more likely to result in an overtly emotional response, for example, with psychological distress and emotional upset. The loss of a father may be more likely to result in an indirect and behavioral expression of emotional upset, such as excess alcohol consumption.

Past social contexts involving childhood and adult experiences with the parent also influence adults' reactions to loss. Some adults who grew up with a father who had a drinking problem actually experience a *reduction* in psychological distress following the father's death. This suggests that the loss of a difficult parent or a parent with a difficult history provides emotional relief for some adults. In these cases, the loss may free the child to move forward and to change in positive or desired ways. But again I find gender differences in that the loss of a difficult parent affects sons and daughters in different ways. For example, although daughters who grew up with difficult fathers are likely to feel psychological relief when their father dies, sons who lose a difficult father are often extremely upset. George is surprised at the extent of his grief following the death of a difficult and violent father:

> He was a very impatient person, explosive, and he could be violent. . . . Most of the times I could hear my parents fight after we went to bed. . . . It was a wood frame house and you could feel it shake, you know. That kind of violence. . . . I know that I'm still resentful of the way he treated me when I was young. . . . I grieved more than I thought I would. . . . There was more sadness to it than I thought there would be. . . . I've often looked at it like I didn't have a father.

In addition, sons with a difficult family history often react to the death in ways that parallel their father's difficulties. Sons whose fathers drank heavily often increase their own alcohol consumption following the death, and sons whose fathers had mental health problems exhibit a greater increase in psychological symptoms than do sons without this difficult history. George was frightened to see more of his father in himself after his father died: "The apple I don't think fell very far from the tree, and it's a shame." In such cases, personal change that parallels the difficult parent's characteristics or behaviors may be viewed as undesirable by the bereaved adult, yet somehow unavoidable. Personal change that results in increasingly difficult behavior may also undermine the adult's close relationships with others.

A difficult father has different implications for sons and daughters, and as a result, a difficult father symbolizes different things for them. Young daughters may have been more likely than young sons to perceive a difficult father as threatening, and in adulthood, daughters are more likely than sons to be responsible for the care of parents. The loss of a difficult father may then symbolize an end to the literal and symbolic threat and responsibility that such fathers pose for daughters. Certainly, several of the daughters I spoke with spent years taking abusive, late-night calls from alcoholic fathers. Lorrie checked on her father daily, did his laundry, and prepared meals for him – despite the fact that he made no attempt to see her when she was a child and treated her horribly during most of their adult encounters. Such women are trapped in the role of the good daughter who should support the father in order to earn love and respect. In contrast, sons feel less responsible for their father and, in turn, may feel less relief when the father dies. However, because sons more strongly identify with the father, they are more likely to emulate him by adopting his problematic personal styles and behaviors.

Nancy Chodorow argues that, from infancy onward, the stage is set for lifelong gender differences in relationships with parents (as well as others).[2] She sees these differences as arising from the gendered identification of children with parents. Chodorow's work emphasizes that early socialization experiences result in more permeable ego boundaries between daughters and parents, especially mothers, and this leads women to feel more responsible for others. Boys, on the other hand, must come to reject their mother and identify with the same-sex parent, their father; this leads boys and men to erect boundaries between themselves and others. My research on parent loss suggests that the identification of children with their same-sex parent, along with the nature of their feelings toward the opposite-sex parent, profoundly influence how adults respond to a parent's death and the ways in which adult identity is altered following a parent's death.

THE SYMBOLIC PARENT

Relationships with parents are laden with symbolic meaning for children. Some parents represent personal validation and belief in the child's success, whereas others represent relentless criticism and belief in the child's inevitable failure. The symbolic meaning of the relationship signifies what the adult loses when a parent dies. These symbolic images of parents also influence how the adult son or daughter responds to the parent's death. Adults who associate a parent with the absence of love have more difficulty after the parent's death than do those without this association. Adults with this symbolic image feel more distressed and less recovered than other bereaved adults. Many of these individuals experience strong grief reactions because they must now cope with the knowledge that they will never be able to obtain the unconditional love or approval that they had always hoped for from their mother or father.

This feeling is most exaggerated in sons who had an alcoholic or mentally unbalanced father and in bereaved adults who had an extremely critical or judgmental parent. Once the parent is gone, problems with the parent may never be fully resolved. The adult may have yearned for this resolution all of his or her life. Mark poignantly describes this pain:

> I think one of the things I miss is not being able to hear him say that he was proud of me. . . . I was always proud of him, but I never heard him say that . . . that won't happen. [*Interviewer*: Were you waiting for him to say it?] Well, I guess more than I thought I was. . . . About a year ago I was watching a TV show called "Major Dad" and Brian Keith was on as the Major's father . . . that was one of the things the Major said to him was, "You never said that you were proud of me." And I was sitting there watching it. You know, tears were just running down my face. . . . I mean, I was a good kid.

Many adults experience strong grief reactions because they must now cope with the knowledge that they will never be able to obtain the love, approval, or stability that they had always hoped for from the parent. George, who strongly identifies with his father, also expresses the pain of this kind of loss: "Other people have fathers that they enjoy. Why couldn't I? . . . I lost the opportunity. Now there's no chance."

In some cases, however, the loss of a critical or judgmental parent can be freeing to the child. For example, for the first time in their lives, Rebecca and Tom felt free to be themselves and leave their unhappy marriages because a critical parent was no longer there to disapprove and cast judgment.

Other symbolic images tend to be associated with more positive adjustment following a parent's death. For example, adults who feel that their parent symbolized a family line – a series of generations that lives on – have less severe grief reactions than adults who do not have this view. Individuals with this symbolic view benefit because they see the parent as living on into the future through successive generations. Bobby, forty-one, describes this passing of the generational torch:

> In general, I understand more about my relationship with my dad now. . . . Losing my dad, my son has been real sweet about it and has prayed for me and the family and Grandpa. . . . There is sort of a chain going on here and so the relationship with my son . . . has become more meaningful.

A growing focus on the next generation can trigger substantial personal change. Some adults make a conscious decision to become a "better" parent or have a different kind of family. Paula, who was raised as a fundamentalist Christian and who learned, only after he died, that her dear father was Jewish, is now devoted to assuming a Jewish identity:

> I started putting together information about half of my being that has been missing. So I've had many pangs of feeling, "Why isn't he here so that I can ask him these questions?" . . . Now, I've converted to Judaism. . . . It's like this is where I belong.

Paula now wants to marry a Jewish man and have her own children who will be raised in a Jewish family.

A NEW ADULT IDENTITY

Most people are fundamentally altered by the loss of a parent. Change may be positive, negative, or neutral from the adult's point of view and from the point of view of those who engage in significant relationships with him or her. However, even those who are emotionally devastated by the loss may perceive some positive consequences as resulting not necessarily from the loss itself but from the process of dealing with the loss. Past interactions with the parent determine the predominant strategies – both conscious and unconscious – for change in the self. Individuals change in order to:

- resolve longstanding issues with the parent;
- hold onto the parent by becoming more like him or her;
- seek posthumous parental approval by becoming more like the person he or she thinks the parent would like;
- break away from the parent by doing things that would have hurt a much-loved parent or upset a critical, judgmental, or disapproving parent; or
- safely reject certain traits, beliefs, or behaviors of the parent.

Grief expert Therese Rando argues that the process of self-change and identification with a deceased person is not pathological if the mourner comprehends that the person is dead, understands the implications of that loss, and moves forward in an adaptive way.[3] In fact, if these conditions are met, identification with the deceased person may actually assist the individual in moving forward. Furthermore, the restructuring and reassembly of self may result in greater maturity or contentment for the individual than experienced in the past. In this sense, the loss provides the opportunity for positive change. On the other hand, a strong tendency to identify with the parent, along with an inability to move forward with one's own life, is indicative of psychological distress that may interfere with adaptive functioning.

In an attempt to make sense of the loss and cope with emotional upset, some adults undergo monumental changes: For example, some adults elect to leave long-term marriages. Others find themselves blossoming at this time because they are liberated from the influence of a critical or unloving parent. At this key turning point in adulthood, life scripts are rewritten to initiate change and to incorporate change.

The death of a parent initiates a rite of passage into a new adult identity. Most adults find a way to view themselves not necessarily as a better person but as a different person – as more responsible, less focused on work, more like or different from their parent, or as a different kind of parent with their own child. The death of a parent transforms the adult child into the adult who is no longer a child – into an adult who glimpses personal mortality and finds a way to become his or her own parent. Greg, age thirty-eight, explains:

> It forced me to grow up emotionally. I am truly a stronger, more understanding, secure person – *most* of the time. I would rather have not had to lose my mother and father to learn those things about myself, but, realistically, I would not have grown if I had not had to.

The loss of the second parent may be particularly likely to evoke this sense of adulthood. Dorie told me: "Losing Mom, after Dad had already been gone almost ten years, made me feel very alone, an orphan. It was a scary feeling." Max said, "I feel more lost and abandoned . . . because now I have no parents. . . . I feel very vulnerable." Generally, I find that the effects of the first and second parent's death are fairly similar, but the feelings of isolation, orphanhood, and a sense of being on one's own are often stronger following the second parent's death.

WORDS OF ENCOURAGEMENT FROM THE BEREAVED

The bereaved often talk about how helpful it is to share their loss with a person who has been through this experience. Ginger explains, "They've felt that same pain." The men and women who I spoke with generously shared their experiences of grief and loss with me. They had several messages they wanted me to deliver to the bereaved about what might be helpful in coping with the loss of a parent. They suggest:

- grieve in your own way;
- rely on relationships with others;
- if possible, resolve issues with parents before they die;
- give up feelings of guilt and regret;
- review the parent's worldly possessions;
- embrace spirituality; and
- seek professional help.

Grieve in Your Own Way

Many of the people I interviewed suggest grieving fully and always keeping in mind that grief is a normal response to loss. Greg, thirty-eight, suggests, "Don't try to not hurt. Take time to think and feel whatever feelings there are." Joel, forty, adds:

> Don't try to keep from crying. It really does feel good. Don't worry if it invades your thoughts. That's natural. Feel your feelings. They're not right or wrong. They're just the way you feel. Don't expect the feeling of loss to completely go away.

Although many adults are vocal about the importance of expressing grief, some find it more helpful to stay busy and avoid thoughts of the parent. Eileen, thirty-eight, explains why staying busy helped her:

> Getting busy again was real helpful. Sitting around the house, if I had taken another week off at home, I might have just kept thinking and thinking and been alone.

Lack of grief expression does not necessarily mean that pent-up emotion will eventually and painfully surface. Psychologist and grief expert Camille Wortman and her colleagues find that those individuals who are least distressed immediately following a young child's death are the same individuals who are least distressed in the months and years following the loss.[4]

Those who have lived through the loss of a parent stress the importance of being true to oneself, whether that means giving in to your feelings of grief and loss or avoiding your feelings. The message is that we should not feel like there is only one appropriate way to deal with this loss. Lynn, fifty-three, tells the newly bereaved what helped her, while emphasizing that everyone has his or her own way of getting through loss:

> I would advise people to feel their feelings, not repress them. I guess if I could have done anything differently that's what I would do. But a lot of that is just your way of coping with things, your personality. You can't suddenly become a different person in order to get through something more easily.

The bereaved often worry that they are not grieving appropriately, that they are too upset or not upset enough, often because others suggest to them that there is a more appropriate way to grieve. In reality, some individuals cope better if they grieve fully and expressively and others cope better if they are able to stay busy and avoid thoughts of the loss.

Relationships with Others

The bereaved emphasize the value of relying on relationships with others. First, they advise those who lose a parent to talk with others about the loss. Bobby, forty-one, advises, "Don't keep it all to yourself; get as much support as you can. Nancy, forty-five, says, "If you need help or a shoulder to cry on, ask for it – don't wait for it to be offered."

Many of the bereaved emphasize the helpfulness of talking with those who have been through a similar loss. In fact, many people find that they develop close and sharing relationships with people they hardly knew before the loss, but who also recently lost a parent.

Some adults find it helpful to consider how their deceased parent would advise them to cope with the loss. Narda, forty-one, found that this advice has helped her immensely, "My brother told me when I was sad one day, 'Mom would not want you to live this way.' I think of that a lot."

Resolve Issues with Parents While They Are Alive

Although I asked men and women to provide advice about dealing with the loss, many of them wanted to provide advice to adults about the period *before the death*. One of the most consistent themes in this regard is to resolve any old issues with the parent, to tell the parent how much they are appreciated, and to say goodbye. Rebecca, forty-one, advises adults:

> To talk with their parents . . . more than talk – listen to and sit down and ask questions and ask them to tell you things about their own growing up and their childhood and their young adult life together so that you can get some sense of where you actually came from . . . because that is a legacy.

Some adults emphasize the importance of spending as much time as possible with the parent when she or he is ill. Jeannie, thirty-one, has regrets about not taking more time off work in the period when her mother was sick: "It killed me to sit at work. . . . My only regret is that I had to sit at my office when my mom was really sick and she really needed me at that point." As we saw earlier, those adults who provide care to a sick parent prior to the loss generally feel few regrets about their parent's final days.

Give Up Feelings of Guilt and Regret

Some have regrets about things that happened in the past relationship with the parent or about the last months or days of the parent's life, and this can make it more difficult to resolve the loss. Cindy, thirty-nine, suggests letting those feelings go:

> Don't feel guilty about the way you feel about things that happened in the past. If you are angry at your deceased parent or didn't say things you wanted to say when they were alive, say them *now* – to someone.

Nathan, twenty-nine, reflects on his experience during the time of his mother's illness:

> I felt guilty for feeling relieved when my mother died. I guess if you realize why you feel relieved it's okay. She is no longer in pain and no longer has to deal with the misery of her disease. Don't feel guilty for feeling that sense of relief.

Some adults suggested making a concerted effort to find out about the parent's wishes about burial, cremation, and property disposition prior to the death and to resolve any property or legal issues. This knowledge can make it easier for the family after the parent dies; it also reassures the family to know that they are carrying out the parent's wishes.

Review the Parent's Worldly Possessions

Although it can be stressful to have to sort through a deceased parent's personal possessions, some adults found it helpful to them in learning to accept and live with the loss. In Valerie Steiker's memoir, she finds an entire family history in the things her parents left behind, and realizes that these "things" chronicle her own development:

> Although I had always known they were keepers, I was nonetheless astounded by all the things my parents had held on to. In one afternoon we'd manage to unearth our childhood collection of tutus, our father's box of penny magic tricks (seemingly untouched since boyhood), and a stack of our mother's old sewing patterns from McCall's.
>
> The most astonishing thing about going on an archeological dig in your own household is that almost everything you find is linked to the development of you.[5]

Dealing with the parent's possessions or property can help the bereaved to feel closer to their parent. Glenn, thirty-nine, regrets losing this opportunity: "Don't let family members throw the parent's things away before you get to see them. . . . I would have wanted some of those things. They meant a lot to me."

Connie, twenty-nine, emphasizes the importance of sorting and distributing property and possessions in a timely manner:

> If you must empty a house or apartment where your parent lived, do so immediately, don't wait. It will be much harder. It sounds awfully callous, but if you know that your parent is dying, talk to the family about what each one wants from the house. It saves a lot of recriminations later to know Aunt Louise always wanted the hall table that you would have donated to Goodwill!

Embrace Spirituality

Some adults recommend relying on spirituality or religious faith to cope with the loss. A belief in the afterlife comforts many and allows them to believe that the deceased is not permanently lost to them. Tina, thirty-five, explains:

> The main comfort for our family has been our faith in God and the fact that we truly believe our parents are in a better place.... It was a comfort to know that they were experiencing death together as they experienced life together for fifty-four years. And now they are in heaven and we know they are watching over us.... I'm going to see my parents again.

Other kinds of spirituality can also comfort the bereaved: Connecting with nature by planting a special tree or hiking in the wilderness can be helpful. One woman told me that she and her siblings camped in the woods and made pancakes for breakfast just like they used to do with their father when they were children. The critical ingredient seems to be finding a spiritual connection to the lost parent.

Other suggestions include spending time at the gravesite and writing one's thoughts about the parent or even writing to the parent. Several people emphasized the importance of taking care of oneself during the grief process. Jackie, thirty-six, suggests, "Be good to yourself. Pamper yourself. Play with your pets. Have fun with your children." Eva, forty-two advises, "Don't make too many demands on yourself at this time."

Seek Professional Help

Relationships with professionals – whether a clinical specialist such as a psychologist or a helping professional such as a religious leader or physician – can be helpful to the bereaved and may even lessen the risk of future psychological problems for individuals who are at high risk following bereavement.[6] Although many of the people in my study felt that they probably would have benefited from professional help following the loss of their parent, most people did not seek it. Yet many of them advise the newly bereaved to talk with a professional. Harper, fifty, advises, "Don't be afraid to get professional help to cope if you need it. You are not a failure to admit you need help."

DIRECTING PERSONAL CHANGE

Although we cannot control who our parent was or how our parent viewed us, we do have some control over how to resolve the loss of our parent and the relationship that we shared.[7] Simply being aware of the factors that underlie personal change gives us the power to channel personal change in desired directions. Yet we should recognize that efforts to change in a particular direction will not always be easy, particularly when past experiences with parents or current social circumstances tend to drive us in the opposite direction. Coming to terms with a parent's death is, to a great degree, about the resolution of childhood issues. Resolution may mean becoming more responsible and mature, but resolution does not necessarily result in inner peace and outer happiness. For example, an individual may adopt the dysfunctional behavior of a deceased parent or leave a loving relationship in an attempt to resolve old issues with the parent. The parent's death fans the flames of family issues so that the desire for resolution is intensified. Yet we can keep in mind that the manner of this resolution shapes the next phase of adulthood by defining how we view ourselves and how we relate to others.

Although grief and loss can be expressed in many different, yet adaptive, ways certain responses to loss can be maladaptive. Adopting a difficult parent's behaviors can be destructive. Drinking to excess can put oneself and others in danger. Extreme anger and aggression can harm loved ones and destroy valued relationships. When we become our difficult parent and this is something we do not want to replicate, it can help to get professional guidance from someone who specializes in grief and loss. When we respond to loss in self-destructive ways or in ways that harm others, or when it seems impossible to go on with life, it is time for help. It does not indicate weakness to get this kind of help. Rather, it signifies self-reflection, insight, and the courage to become the kind of adult we truly want to be.

ADVICE TO THOSE ASSISTING THE BEREAVED

Many of the men and women I spoke with also had strong advice for those who want to help the bereaved. They suggest:

- don't give advice,
- listen, and
- acknowledge the loss.

The adults I spoke with stressed the importance of *not* giving advice to the bereaved. More specifically, they do not want to be told how they should feel or how to grieve. Rebecca, forty-one, emphasizes, "Don't give advice. . . . It would be better if they would listen. If they would just sit down and say, 'How do you feel right now?' " Similarly, Matt, thirty-two, suggests focusing on feelings, not advice: "There's nothing really that they can do unless they've experienced the same thing. Then they can tell them how they felt. . . . But I think basically do not offer advice."

The bereaved often feel that it is presumptuous for others to tell them how to deal with loss. It can be especially upsetting when others pressure them to recover quickly.[8]

On the other hand, it can be very helpful to have someone simply listen. Dan, twenty-five, tells those who want to help:

> If you've never lost a parent of your own, try, try, try to understand what it must be like. . . . Don't say the old cliché stuff. Just listen. Ask some questions about the person who died. Try to get to know that person.

Most said they wanted to talk about their deceased parent, at least occasionally. Yet they sometimes had the impression that others did not want to talk about them. Abigail, forty-four, describes how some of her friends and coworkers reacted to her loss:

> People didn't really want to hear about him. . . . They reserve their sympathies for what they consider to be more tragic losses – such as that of a spouse or child or young adult. People just didn't seem willing to express much sympathy over the death of an older person.

Sometimes, listening to the bereaved means being comfortable with their expression of emotion. The presence of a caring person or a hand on a shoulder can be gifts to the bereft.

It can also be very helpful to the bereaved when others ac-knowledge the importance of the deceased parent's life and the significance of the death. A very simple and helpful way to ac-complish this is to attend the funeral or memorial service of the deceased and/or to send a personal note or condolence card. This may seem like a small gesture, but it can mean a lot. Judy, fifty-seven, describes how the funeral of her father helped her:

> At the funeral in the small town, we had so many people that it was just overflowing. . . . There were so many things that people came and told me about my father . . . little things that my father had done and . . . how he did things for them that I did not know about. Oh, it was wonderful.

Conversely, when certain close individuals do not appear at the funeral, the bereaved person may be quite upset by their ab-sence. Angie, twenty-nine, tells how the absence of her friends affected her:

> It has been real hard for me to accept the lack of sup-port I've had from my good friends. They did not attend the funeral. . . . I couldn't imagine my mother's death not meaning that much to them. . . . It has made it harder for me to deal with her passing. I have grown resentful of them for that.

Several men and women told me that they were deeply moved by a few words of support from friends or even minor acquain-tances. Some adults received notes or letters from old friends of the deceased parent with messages about the type of person the parent had been or things the parent had accomplished in life.

These messages reinforce the adult's view of their parent as a special person and may give the adult a glimpse of parts of the parent's life with which they had been largely unfamiliar. A few people decided to compile a memory book about their parent and solicited memories from friends and relatives about the parent for the book. This exercise was deeply rewarding to those who pursued it.

Unhelpful Advice

Many of us are uncomfortable dealing with death and loss, and although we want to help the bereaved, we hesitate. We may fear that we will upset the bereaved person. While most people do want to have the opportunity to talk about their loss, they do not want to be compelled to confront it at every turn. Moreover, they do not want to hear that the loss was "for the best" regardless of the parent's illness or age. Desley, fifty-three, explains:

> People don't expect older adults to grieve for an older parent that's died.... What I had was a lot of, "Oh, but she was seventy-five years old." It doesn't matter; the age doesn't matter.... I kept being told, "Well, you know she's better off." This is true, but it doesn't affect how you feel.

Those who wish to help the bereaved should be careful not to minimize the loss of a parent. Tina, thirty-five, advises:

> Don't try to rationalize death and say, "Well, we all lose our parents," or "At least it wasn't your husband or wife." ... Just understand that it's very profound.

RECOVERY AND RESOLUTION

Regrets about the past, unresolved issues with the parent, and negative symbolic images of the parent complicate recovery from the loss of a parent. However, most individuals, over time, find a way to cope with the loss. This does not mean that individuals quickly recover and go on as they did before. In fact, the loss can evoke considerable change and may never be fully resolved. Terri, thirty-four, explains:

> Everybody wants to tell you that everything will be fine and time will heal this . . . but my life will never be the same. That doesn't mean it won't be good or fulfilling or happy, but it's not going to be the same.

On the other hand, most individuals do find happiness and fulfillment in their lives following a parent's death and time does seem to help. I asked adults how recovered they felt at different points in time following their parent's death. On average, they experienced steady improvement in feelings of recovery. Although the national survey data reveal that the adverse consequences of parent loss are apparent up to three years following the loss, these effects are not apparent five years later.[9] At this point, adults who lost a parent exhibit levels of alcohol consumption and psychological distress that are similar to their nonbereaved counterparts. The bereaved actually exhibit *better* physical health than the non-bereaved eight years after the parent's death. Improved physical health makes sense in light of the health behavior changes that some of the bereaved exhibited shortly following their parent's death. Facing mortality and, in turn, improving one's health by losing weight, quitting smoking, or starting regular exercise can have long-term benefits for physical health.

It is important to bear in mind that, although a parent's death may initially evoke considerable upset in adults, over time, most adults experience change in the self and in their family – changes that allow them to move forward, often in positive and adaptive ways.

A Relationship That Never Ends

Many adults maintain an ongoing relationship with their parent, even after the parent dies. Contacts beyond death typically occur not in the form of apparitions but in more subtle ways. For example, Jeannie, thirty-one, described how she turned on the radio and found that it was on a Spanish-language station. This was a sign to Jeannie that her mother, a former Spanish teacher, was trying to comfort and communicate with Jeannie.

Some adults begin to recognize the parent in their own values, attitudes, or behaviors, while others actually change to become more like the parent. Kim's parents remain with her, in part, because they remain within her:

> I used to think, "Well, death – that's the end of every-
> thing." But it's not. . . . I feel like my parents are still here
> spiritually in the things that they taught me and I see them
> coming out in myself. I guess it was about a year ago or
> so, I was cleaning house and I have two cats and I started
> singing to my cats and I started laughing and then I started
> crying because my mom was an animal lover and I used to
> get so aggravated with her when I was growing up because

she would talk to the animals – and I realized that I was doing what she did. . . . Sometimes, I would say a phrase and it would be something that my father would say and I would think, "Oh my God, I'm becoming my parents." But then again, it's kind of comforting.

Since the loss of her parents, Kim has adopted many of their habits and mannerisms, and she has even come to embrace them. Others identify with their parent in more dramatic ways. For example, Tom, who pitied his father for spending so many years in a miserable marriage, felt good for his father as well as himself when he left his own marriage following his father's death.

Some adults continue to visit the gravesite or some symbolic location that makes them feel closer to the parent. Veronica, thirty-nine, finds her father in the night sky:

Every night I go outside and look at the sky. There's a certain star I find and I like to believe that's him – sometimes it has a red twinkle and that was his favorite color. I talk to him – sometimes cry, sometimes not. . . . Every now and then I have a very realistic dream where I can feel him hug me.

Many adults continue to talk to the parent or, when faced with difficult decisions or under stress, to consider what the parent would tell them to do in these circumstances. Kim, like many bereaved adults who were close to their parents, feels that her parents continue to look after her even in death:

The week after my mom died I had to take my finals. I was scared to death . . . and I was panicking. . . . All of a sudden there was a feeling of a hand on my shoulder and this total calm. I picked up my pencil and I just did the test. . . . I don't even remember any of the questions but my dad always helped me through my math problems . . . and that's how I worked through it.

Kim feels that her father is her "guardian angel." She often goes to the cemetery where her parents are buried and talks with them about her problems, just as she did when they were living. These visits calm and comfort her. She often leaves feeling more certain about what decisions she should make.

Some adults see their own children as carrying on their parent's legacy. Others do not feel that the parent is forever lost or even missing; they expect to see him or her again in the afterlife. This thought comforts Lynn: "My religious beliefs have sustained me because I don't feel like physical death is the end of life. I know that my mother still lives somewhere else."

A striking characteristic of interviews with the bereaved is their tendency to speak of the deceased parent in the present tense. At first I found this to be disconcerting. Now, with the benefit of several years of research, I think that this tendency is simply a reflection of the larger phenomenon of keeping the parent present in this world. It is difficult for most of us to relinquish this relationship. For better or for worse, our parents never fully leave us behind.

I asked bereaved adults how close they felt to their parent at various points in the life course: during childhood, the teen years, early and late adulthood, and even following the parent's death.[10] Following a dip in the teen years, adult children feel increasingly close to their parents as they age. Perhaps most remarkably, adults report feeling closer to their parent after the parent dies than at any previous point in the life course.

The relationship between parent and child continues throughout our lives, even after our parent dies. The death of a parent is a powerful, transformative moment in the ebb and flow of life. From this painful loss can emerge transcendence to a new adult identity.

APPENDIX

DATA AND MEASURES

THE NATIONAL SURVEY

Data

The national data reported in Chapters 2, 5, and 6 are from a two-wave panel survey of individuals, ages twenty-four to ninety-six, in the contiguous United States.[1] This survey, supported by the National Institute on Aging (AGO5562) and conducted by the Survey Research Center of the University of Michigan, was designed to assess issues of health, productivity, and social relationships over the life course. I worked with the original research team at the University of Michigan in formulating questions on family relationships for this national survey. Face-to-face interviews, lasting approximately ninety minutes each, were conducted with individuals in 1986 ($N = 3,617$) and 1989 ($N = 2,867$). Between 1986 and 1989, 207 adults in the sample experienced the death of a biological parent. I compared this group of individuals with 1,210 individuals who had at least one living biological parent and had not experienced a parent's death between 1986 and 1989. All individuals in both groups were interviewed in 1986 and 1989. Individuals who did not meet the criteria for inclusion in one of the two groups were excluded from the analyses. This reduced the sample size for analysis to 1,417 for the analyses reported in

Chapter 2: 1,407 respondents were excluded because both parents died prior to 1986; thirty were excluded because they experienced the death of a stepparent; and thirteen were excluded because of missing data on the parent's status.

The attrition rate between the 1986 and 1989 interviews was 21 percent ($N = 750$). Twenty-two percent of that attrition ($N = 166$) is due to mortality of respondents; the remaining attrition ($N = 584$) is due to nonresponse. Excluding deceased respondents, nonrespondents are more likely to be black, male, never married, and of low socioeconomic status, and to exhibit higher scores on psychological distress and alcohol consumption. Individuals who are more likely to be distressed by a parent's death may have been more likely to drop out of the study; this could result in *underestimation* of the impact of a parent's death for some groups. Differences in the dependent variables are less important because I am assessing *change* in the dependent variable over time. I had no information on whether respondents who lost a parent after 1986 were more or less likely to drop out of the survey. Nonrespondents did not differ from respondents on any of the measures of relationships with parents in 1986. A follow-up interview was conducted in 1994, and these results are reported in Chapter 9.

The subsample analyzed for Chapter 5 on marital and cohabiting relationships includes 123 consistently married/cohabiting individuals who lost a biological parent between 1986 and 1989 and a comparison group of 679 married/cohabiting individuals who had at least one living biological parent in 1989 and who had not experienced the death of a parent between 1986 and 1989. The married/cohabiting selection criteria were that all respondents had been living with their partner for at least six months prior to the 1986 interview and remained in the same relationship through the 1989 interview. Only 3 percent of the subsample

were cohabiting rather than married. I refer to marital relationships and marital quality in the text in order to simplify discussion.
All analyses include a control variable to indicate married versus
cohabiting status (0 = cohabiting, 1 = married).

The analysis reported in Chapter 6 on relationships with children is based on a subsample of individuals who have children. Of
the bereaved individuals, 184 have a child of any age; 143 have
at least one child age sixteen or older. The comparison group of
nonbereaved individuals includes those persons who have at least
one living biological parent and at least one child ($N = 1,274$).

The 1994 results reported in Chapter 9 use the same statistical
method as described above except that the dependent variable was
the 1994 value.

Measures

DEATH OF A PARENT. In 1989, respondents were asked whether a
biological mother or father had died since the time of the first interview. Between 1986 and 1989, 112 adult children experienced
the death of a mother, eighty-eight experienced the death of a
father, and seven had lost both parents. The bereavement variables include a dummy variable for mother's death (1 = mother
died, 0 = otherwise) and father's death (1 = father died, 0 =
otherwise). A mother's death and a father's death are assessed
separately in Chapters 2 and 5 because additional analyses indicate that the two types of death have different effects on mental
and physical health outcomes and marital relationships. Mother
death and father death are not coded separately in Chapter 5 because analyses reveal no difference in the effects of a mother's or
a father's death on relationships with children. In Chapter 6, bereavement is coded 0 for those individuals who did not experience

the death of a parent between 1986 and 1989 and 1 for individuals who experienced the death of a parent during this time. I also include a variable for length of time bereaved (found to be nonsignificant in the previous analyses) in Chapter 6. Length of time bereaved is measured in number of months since the death. Length of time bereaved ranges from one to thirty-one months (mean = fifteen months).

DEMOGRAPHIC CHARACTERISTICS. Demographic variables include gender, race, marital status (married, divorced or separated, widowed, and never married; married constituted the omitted category in regression analyses), age, family income, and years of education.

In the analyses of marital relationships, reported in Chapter 5, marital status is not included as a control variable since the focus is only on married/cohabiting relationships. In Chapter 5, additional control variables are included for cohabiting status and number of years married (mean = 19.2, s.d. = 11.99).

QUALITY OF ADULT RELATIONSHIP WITH PARENTS. Adult parent-child relationships were assessed by asking respondents several questions about the quality of their relationships with living mothers and fathers in 1986. A measure of *emotional support* from parents was comprised of two questions: "How much does your (mother/father) make you feel loved and cared for?" and "How much is your (mother/father) willing to listen when you need to talk about your worries or problems?" (mother $\alpha = .71$, father $\alpha = .74$). A measure of *relationship strain* was comprised of two questions: "How much do you feel your (mother/father) makes too many demands on you?" and "How much is your (mother/father) critical of you or what you do?" (mother $\alpha = .65$, father

$\alpha = .74$). Each of these questions includes five response categories from which respondents chose one: "a great deal, quite a bit, some, a little, or not at all." *Parent's impairment* prior to death was measured by asking respondents, "Was your (mother/father) mentally and physically capable of giving advice or help if you need it?" ("no" or "yes"). *Frequency of contact* was measured by asking, "During the past 12 months, how often did you have contact with your (mother/father) – either in person, by phone, or by mail? Would you say more than once a week, once a week, 2 or 3 times a month, about once a month, less than once a month or never?"

CHILDHOOD MEMORIES OF PROBLEM PARENTS. Respondents were asked retrospective questions about childhood experiences with their parents: (1) "While you were growing up, did anyone in your home have a *serious drinking problem*? (2) What about a *mental health problem*? (3) Was anyone *violent*?" ("yes"or "no," for each question). Respondents were asked to indicate whether it was the mother or father who exhibited these problems.

DEPENDENT VARIABLES: MEASURES OF WELL-BEING. *Psychological distress* is measured with an eleven-item version of the Center for Epidemiological Studies Depression Scale (CES-D). The CES-D demonstrates high reliability and validity in community surveys and is widely accepted among epidemiologists as a measure of psychological distress in general populations.[2] Respondents were asked how often they experienced each of the following in the past week: "I felt depressed"; "I felt lonely"; "people were unfriendly"; "I enjoyed life"; "I did not feel like eating, my appetite was poor"; "I felt sad"; "I felt that people disliked me"; "I could not get going"; "I felt that everything I did was an effort"; "my sleep was restless"; and "I was happy" (1986 $\alpha = .89$, 1989 $\alpha = .82$).

A standard approach to measuring alcohol consumption involves assessing both the frequency and volume of consumption.[3] In my study, *alcohol consumption* was measured by multiplying the number of days per month that respondents drank by the number of drinks that respondents typically consumed on those days.

Self-reports of *physical health status* were obtained from respondents by asking, "How would you rate your health at the present time? Would you say it is excellent, very good, good, fair, or poor?"

DEPENDENT VARIABLES: MEASURES OF MARITAL QUALITY. Respondents were asked a number of questions about their marital/ cohabiting relationships. I assess emotional support from one's partner, relationship strain, partner's negative behaviors, relationship harmony, frequency of conflict, and frequency of feeling bothered by the relationship. The *emotional support* ($\alpha = .70$) and *relationship strain* ($\alpha = .64$) questions parallel the emotional support and strain questions assessed for parent-child relationships and described above.

Relationship harmony ($\alpha = .67$) is based on responses to three statements: (1) "My (spouse/partner) doesn't treat me as well as I deserve to be treated"; (2) "I sometimes think of divorcing or separating from my (spouse/partner)"; (3) "There have been things that have happened in our (marriage/relationship) that I can never forgive." Response options are "strongly agree," "agree somewhat," "disagree somewhat," or "strongly disagree." *Partner's negative behavior* ($\alpha = .44$) indicates exposure to particularly problematic behaviors of a partner that typically impose strain on a relationship. This index is based on four statements: (1) "My (spouse/partner) drinks too much"; (2) "(He/she) pushes, slaps, or hits me"; (3) "(He/she) wastes money the family needs for other things"; and (4) "(He/she) has extramarital affairs." Individuals were asked to indicate how often their spouse/partner engages in these behaviors; response options are "never," "often," or "sometimes." *Frequency of conflict* with one's partner is evaluated with the following question: "How often would you say the two of you typically have unpleasant disagreements or conflict?" Response options are "daily or almost daily," "two or three times a week," "almost once a week," "two or three times a month," "almost once a month," "less than once a month," or "never." *Frequency of feeling bothered* by the relationship was assessed with the following question: "Taking everything into consideration, how often do you feel bothered or upset by your (marriage/relationship)?" Response options include "almost always," "often," "sometimes," "rarely," or "never."

DEPENDENT VARIABLES: RELATIONSHIPS WITH CHILDREN. I consider four measures of quality of relationships with children. These measures are obtained by asking parents about their relationships with their children: (1) *emotional support* provided by children to parents, (2) *relationship strain* imposed by children on parents, (3) *parental dissatisfaction*, and (4) *frequency of contact* with nonresidential children aged sixteen and older. Questions used to construct emotional support, relationship strain, and frequency of contact parallel those described above for other relationships. Parental dissatisfaction is indicated by satisfaction with being a parent, how happy respondents are with the way their children turned out, and how often they feel bothered or upset as a parent.

All measures are coded so that higher values indicate higher levels of the construct being measured. All scales are constructed by taking the mean of the items used to build the index and standardizing the index.

METHODS FOR ASSESSING THE EFFECTS
OF A PARENT'S DEATH

I compared the dependent variables of adults who experienced the death of a parent between 1986 and 1989 with those of adults who did not have this experience. I accomplish this by regressing the 1989 values for the dependent variables (e.g., CES-D scores, physical health status, or alcohol consumption) on the bereavement variables, the demographic variables, and the 1986 value of the dependent variable. Controlling for the 1986 value on the dependent variable allowed me to assess the amount of change in the dependent variable over time.

I also assessed a number of factors that might modify an adult's reaction to a parent's death. For example, the effect of a parent's death on mental health sometimes depends on demographic characteristics of adults or the prior quality of the relationship with the parent. I tested a series of intermediate models to derive final models. First, a separate equation is estimated for each two-way interaction between bereavement and a possible modifying variable (interactions are assessed between possible modifiers and a mother's death and between possible modifiers and a father's death in Chapters 2 and 5; interactions between possible modifiers and a parent's death (mother or father) are assessed in Chapter 6). This involves regressing the 1989 value of the dependent variable on the bereavement variables, a modifying variable, an interaction term between bereavement and a modifying variable, the demographic variables, and the 1986 value of the dependent variable. Missing data were handled by including control variables to indicate the availability of data on specific variables. Where more than one interaction significantly ($p < .05$) predicted a dependent variable, additional equations were estimated that include all significant interactions to determine whether a particular interaction predominates as the source of the effect.

In Chapter 2, I also test for several three-way interactions involving bereavement, measures of prior relationships with parents, and the respondent's gender to consider whether the modifying effects of prior relationships with parents operate the same way for sons and daughters. I use the basic model resulting from the procedures described above as the baseline model. I then apply the same estimation procedures that I used to assess two-way interactions to test possible three-way interactions to derive the most parsimonious final models. The final models include all significant interaction terms, controls for their component variables and lower-order interactions, the basic set of demographic variables, and the 1986 value on the dependent variable. I then calculate predicted values on the dependent variables, net of the 1986 value, for bereaved and nonbereaved respondents in relevant subgroups. More detailed technical information on analyses and results can be found in some of my previous articles on this subject.[4]

A Note on Adult Child/Parent Relationship Results

In the national survey, the death of a parent – whether a mother or a father – seems to have little impact on the amount of emotional support that surviving parents provide to adult children, the amount of strain characterizing the relationship, or how often the parent and child are in contact with one another. The qualitative analysis, however, suggests that this is not necessarily because the death of a parent never affects relationships with surviving parents, but because the death of a parent leads to positive change in relationships with some surviving parents and negative change in relationships with other surviving parents. The national results may include relationships characterized by negative change and relationships characterized by positive change, and by combining all relationships, I may cancel out any evidence of change that does exist. In fact, the local survey provided some support for this possibility in that some relationships are largely unchanged by the loss, other relationships improve, and still other relationships deteriorate. The qualitative analysis suggests that for those respondents for whom there is substantial change in the relationship with a surviving parent, this change often has significant consequences.

IN-DEPTH INTERVIEWS AND THE MAIL SURVEY

Sample

In-depth interviews were conducted with seventy-three individuals, aged twenty-five to sixty-seven, who recently experienced the death of a parent. Respondents for the in-depth interviews were recruited through an article in the major newspaper in an urban/suburban metropolitan area in the Southwestern United States (population of 781,752). Approximately 250 people called to volunteer for participation in the study. Individuals were selected for in-depth interviewing on the basis of length of time bereaved, age, gender, race, and marital status, in an attempt to collect information from a diverse group of individuals. Of those individuals scheduled to be interviewed, only three failed to attend the interview. The mean length of time bereaved in the in-depth interview sample was 12.8 months, with a range of one to forty-four months. Only four respondents were bereaved for longer than thirty-six months. The mean age of respondents was 39.8;

58.9 percent were female; 59.2 percent were married; 87.3 percent were white; 5.6 percent were African American; 7 percent classified themselves in another racial/ethnic category; and the mean annual family income was in the range of $30,000 to $39,999. Face-to-face interviews lasted about seventy minutes on average. Most of the interview was comprised of open-ended questions. Open-ended questions focused on the adult child's past relationship with the deceased parent, as well as the nature of the death and the respondent's personal and social experiences following the loss. Closed-ended questions, asked at the end of the interview, provided additional information on psychological functioning and recovery following the loss. Interviews were conducted between October 1 and December 15, 1993.

All individuals who volunteered to participate in the in-depth interview study but were not included in the in-depth interview sample were later mailed a questionnaire for a small, local survey. I carried out this survey in order to more fully address questions raised in the in-depth interviews and to provide an extra sense of security about the validity of results from the in-depth interview study. Questionnaires were mailed to 208 potential respondents and 123 questionnaires were returned, for a response rate of 59 percent. In mail surveys, a response rate of 50 percent is "adequate" and a rate of 60 percent is "good."[5] The pool of 208 respondents represents the 177 individuals who initially called in response to my request for respondents for in-depth interviews (but who were not included in the in-depth interview sample) as well as an additional thirty-one individuals who called at some point in the following two months to request participation in the study. The mean length of time bereaved for respondents in the mail survey was 17.8 months with a range from one month to sixty months.

The mean age of survey respondents was 41.6 years; the mean annual income was in the range of $30,000 to $39,999 ; 78.9 percent were female; 68.9 percent were married; 96.7 percent were white; 1.6 percent were African American; and 1.6 percent self-identified with some other race/ethnicity.

Of the seventy-three individuals in in-depth interviews, forty-two (58 percent) were married or in a significant relationship prior to the death. Those who were involved in an intimate relationship were asked to describe how their partner behaved following the loss, how the relationship changed as a result of the loss, and how the relationship has affected their recovery from bereavement. Of the 119 individuals included in the local survey, 83 percent were married or in a significant relationship at the time of their parent's death. These individuals were asked a number of closed-ended questions about marital quality. These questions are modeled after those used in the national survey, except that respondents were asked to report on the quality of their marriage *during the first weeks and months following the parent's death.* They were asked an additional question following each of the marital quality questions: "Was this typical of your relationship or did it change after the loss? Would you say it was typical, changed for the better, or changed for the worse?" Since marital relationships vary in quality and I do not have reports of marital quality obtained prior to the loss or reports from a nonbereaved control group for comparison, I asked this question in an attempt to determine whether the respondent feels that the death led to change in the overall quality of the relationship.

Following these questions on relationship change, local survey respondents were asked to write a response, of any length, indicating how they felt their relationship was affected by the loss.

Closed-Ended Questions in In-Depth Interviews and the Local Survey

At the end of in-depth interviews, interviewees were asked a series of closed-ended questions regarding their demographic characteristics, psychological functioning, and recovery. These same questions were also asked in the local survey.

Self-reported recovery is measured with the following item in the local survey: "Please describe how much you feel you have recovered from your (mother/father's) death." Response options are: "completely recovered, almost completely recovered, somewhat recovered, not too recovered, and not at all recovered" (coded 1–5, with higher values indicating more recovery). Responses to the recovery question in the in-depth interviews were obtained by having respondents graph their level of recovery at different points in time following the loss. I coded the most recent entry in order to obtain values for self-reported recovery.

Psychological distress was measured with the CES-D scale, as used in the national survey. Demographic information was obtained for gender, income, education, age, parental status, and marital status.

CLOSENESS TO THE PARENT. One of the major discussion points in in-depth interviews concerned the nature of the past relationship with the parent. Near the end of the interview, I asked each individual how close he or she felt to his or her parent at various points in the life course by plotting degree of closeness to the parent on a graph. This graph juxtaposed degree of closeness with different points in the life course, including the respondents' childhood years, teen years, early adulthood, late adulthood, and after the parent's death.

Measures: Open-Ended Questions

I explored various approaches to obtaining information about the *symbolic meaning* of parents for Chapter 3 and found that one particular open-ended question elicited a range of rich responses. I asked individuals in in-depth interviews, "Overall, what do you feel you lost with the death of your parent?" This question was typically asked toward the middle or end of the interview. Respondents seemed to have an immediate grasp of the question and had no difficulty verbalizing what they lost when their parent died. They often used the word "meaning" and referred to what their parent "meant" to them in their responses. An analysis of the responses to this question along with the original intent in designing the question persuades me that the question does tap into what the parent symbolized to the child. Respondents in the mail survey were asked to respond to a similar open-ended question about symbolic meanings. One concern with this approach to obtaining information about symbolic meanings is that the question wording might elicit primarily positive responses from respondents. My own analysis indicates that although negative meanings do arise in response to this question, they are often couched in terms of missed opportunities to have certain positive themes in relationships with parents. To identify other general themes of symbolic meaning that were not mentioned in response to the specific symbolic meaning question, I conducted an extensive analysis of symbolic meaning themes in the in-depth interviews in their entirety. As Sheldon Stryker has argued, individuals are not necessarily aware of the nature of their role identities, therefore it is not surprising that symbolic meanings of those identities are revealed in the unfolding of the larger interview of roles and relationships rather than in response to one direct question.[6] I also reviewed responses to all of the other open-ended questions in the survey sample to more fully evaluate possible negative symbolic meanings in that sample.

At the end of each series of closed-ended questions about *relationship change*, local survey respondents were asked to describe the most significant changes in their relationships. For example, I asked, "If there have been changes in your sibling relationships that I have not mentioned or that have been very significant for you, please describe those changes." The same question was asked about relationships with surviving parents, children, and spouses/intimate partners.

Relationships were assessed in in-depth interviews either as the respondent chose to raise and discuss them or in response to a general question about relationships following the loss. Relationship issues were raised at different and multiple points by respondents throughout the interview.

Qualitative Methods

Qualitative results reported throughout the book are based on the in-depth interviews as well as open-ended responses from the local survey sample. In-depth interviews were tape recorded and transcribed for analysis. Qualitative data were coded according to the principles outlined by C. Marshall and G. B. Rossman.[7] At least two interviewers, including myself, reviewed each transcript several times and identified general themes associated with bereavement experiences. These themes were entered into a computer database and illustrative quotes were entered under appropriate themes. Where appropriate, themes were cross-listed. Open-ended responses from the local survey are analyzed following the same procedures as used for analysis of the in-depth interview data.

Quotes presented in the text to illustrate major themes from the qualitative analysis are derived from the in-depth interviews and open-ended responses from the local survey.

The results reported in Chapter 3 on symbolic meaning are based on a regression analysis of the combined in-depth interview and local survey data. Themes of symbolic meaning identified in in-depth interviews and in open-ended responses to the local survey were identified and coded so that information on symbolic meaning could be considered in a quantitative analysis (the technical aspects of this analysis are reported in a 1997 article in *Journal of Personal and Social Relationships*).[8] In initial analyses, I evaluated the in-depth interview and survey samples separately. The overall pattern of results did not differ across data sets; however, I conducted an additional analysis that included a control variable indicating whether the respondent was from the in-depth interview sample or the survey sample. This variable was not significant in predicting the dependent variables of psychological distress and self-reported recovery levels. I estimated a series of models in order to derive the most parsimonious models possible in predicting psychological distress and recovery (separate models were derived for each of the two dependent variables). I began by regressing the depression and recovery measures on all of the symbolic meaning themes and the demographic variables. In the next step of the analysis, variables that were significant predictors ($p < .10$) of the dependent variables were retained as a base model. Forward entry (based on criteria pin $= .1$ and pout $= .11$) was then used to enter nonsignificant variables from the original model in order to obtain a parsimonious model. The results reported are from the final parsimonious regression models.

NOTES

CHAPTER 1

1   D. J. Levinson, C. M. Darrow, E. B. Klein, M. H. Levinson, and B. McKee, "The psychosocial development of men in early adulthood and the mid-life transition," in D. F. Richs, A. Thomas, and M. Roth, eds., *Life History Research in Psychotherapy*, vol. 3 (Minneapolis: University of Minnesota Press, 1974), p. 250.

2   R. Davis-Floyd, *Birth as an American Rite of Passage* (Berkeley: University of California Press, 1992), p. 19.

3   I compared bereaved individuals (bereaved within the previous thirty-six months) with nonbereaved individuals on amount of change in their overall levels of psychological distress, physical health, and alcohol consumption over time. By including a nonbereaved group for comparison, I can ascertain whether change in mental and physical health and alcohol consumption is directly linked to a parent's death. Information on the national survey data and measures as well as the statistical techniques for the analysis of these data is available in the appendix. Some of the material presented in this chapter was previously reported in D. Umberson and M. Chen, "Effects of a parent's death on adult children: Relationship salience and reactions to loss," *American Sociological Review* 59 (1994): 152–168.

4   See the Appendix for information on in-depth interview and mail survey samples.

CHAPTER 2

1   From Anna Quindlen, *One True Thing* (New York: Random House, 1994), p. 350. Reprinted with the permission of Random House, Inc. Copyright © 1994 by Anna Quindlen.

2   M. M. Moss and S. Z. Moss, "The impact of parental death on middle aged children," *Omega* 14 (1983–4): 65–75.

3   H. H. Winsborough, L. L. Bumpass, and W. S. Aquilino, *The Death of Parents and the Transition to Old Age*, Working Paper NSFH-39 (Madison: University of Wisconsin, Center for Demography and Ecology, 1991). The experience of parent loss that we see in data from the United States may be different in countries with cultural values and demographic patterns (e.g., shorter life expectancy) that differ from those found in Western, industrialized countries.

4   Developmental psychologists emphasize the importance of midlife as a period of increasing self-reflection. See discussions in E. H. Erikson, *Childhood and Society*, 2nd ed. (New York: Norton, 1963); D. J. Levinson, *The Seasons of a Man's Life* (New York: Knopf, 1974); G. E. Vaillant, *Adaptation to Life* (Boston: Little, Brown, 1977); and D. P. McAdams and E. de St. Aubin, "A theory of generativity and its assessment through self-report, behavioral acts, and narrative themes in autobiography," *Journal of Personality and Social Psychology* 62 (1992): 1003–1015.

5   G. H. Elder, Jr., and A. M. O'Rand, "Adult lives in a changing society," in K. S. Cook, G. A. Fine, and J. S. House, eds., *Sociological Perspectives in Social Psychology* (Needham Heights, Mass.: Allyn and Bacon, 1995), pp. 452–475.

6   Life course researchers emphasize the importance of turning points in adulthood, but, as sociologist Linda George points out, little evidence exists concerning the most important turning points of adulthood. See L. K. George, "Sociological perspectives on life transitions," *Annual Review of Sociology* 19 (1993): 353–373.

7   B. Wheaton and I. Gotlib, "Trajectories and turning points over the life course: Concepts and themes," in I. H. Gotlib and B. Wheaton, eds., *Stress and Adversity Over the Life Course* (Cambridge: Cambridge University Press, 1997), p. 1.

8   See reviews of evidence linking stress to specific health outcomes in S. Cohen and G. M. Williamson, "Stress and infectious disease in humans," *Psychological Bulletin* 98 (1991): 310–357, and S. E. Taylor in *Health Psychology*, 3rd ed. (New York: McGraw-Hill, 1995).

9   We know much more about the impact of specific life events on overall levels of psychological well-being than we do about the processes through which life events have these effects. See a discussion in D. H. Demo, "The self-concept over time: Research issues and directions," *Annual Review of Sociology* 18 (1992): 303–326, and L. K. George, "Sociological perspectives on life transitions," *Annual Review of Sociology* 19 (1993): 353–373. The present work is focused on identifying not only the statistical effects

of parent loss on health and well-being, but also the underlying processes through which a parent's death comes to have these effects. Part of my argument is that the distress associated with the death of a parent propels personal change following the event. Also see J. Kiecolt, "Stress and the decision to change oneself: A theoretical model," *Social Psychology Quarterly* 57 (1994): pp. 49–63.

10 E. Becker, *The Denial of Death* (New York: Free Press, 1973).

11 For example, research shows that women are more likely than men to respond to stress with depression, while men are more likely to report an increase in alcohol use. See a review in S. Rosenfield, "Splitting the difference: Gender, the self, and mental health," in C. S. Aneshensel and J. C. Phelan, eds., *Handbook of the Sociology of Mental Health* (New York: Kluwer Academic/Plenum, 1999), pp. 209–224.

12 The effects of parent loss on mental and physical health and alcohol consumption that are reported in this chapter are based on a longitudinal analysis of national data. For information on sampling, measurement, and statistical methods, see the Appendix. The statistical effects reported in this chapter were originally published in D. Umberson and M. D. Chen, "Effects of a parent's death on adult children: Relationship salience and reaction to loss," *American Sociological Review* 59 (1994): 152–169.

13 From Jeanette Winterson's novel, *Written on the Body* (New York: Random House, 1992), p. 155. Reprinted with the permission of International Creative Management, Inc. Copyright © 1992 by Great Moments Ltd.

14 John Bowlby integrates psychoanalytic theory with ethology to explain why attachment objects, especially mothers, provide a base of security for children. See John Bowlby, *Attachment and Loss*, vol. 1: *Attachment* (Harmondsworth: Pelican Books, 1969), and *Attachment and Loss*, vol. 3: *Loss: Sadness and Depression* (Harmondsworth: Pelican Books, 1980). Bowlby argues that when a child feels threatened by abandonment or withdrawal of the attachment object, this evokes a strong and primitive emotional reaction. See a summary of Bowlby's work as it relates to bereavement in W. Stroebe and M. S. Stroebe, *Bereavement and Health: The Psychological and Physical Consequences of Partner Loss* (Cambridge: Cambridge University Press, 1987).

15 N. Chodorow, *The Reproduction of Mothering* (Berkeley: University of California Press, 1978).

16 S. L. Nock and P. W. Kingston conducted a time-use study showing the relative amounts of time that men and women spend on childcare, housework, and paid work in "Time with children: The impact of couples' work-time commitments," *Social Forces* 67 (1988): 59–85. See additional information on gender and childcare in B. A. Shelton, *Women,*

Men, and Time: Gender Differences in Paid Work, Housework, and Leisure (New York, Greenwood Press, 1992), and R. C. Barnett, "Gender, high- and low-schedule-control, housework tasks, and psychological distress," Journal of Family Issues 18 (1997): 794–806. In Of Human Bonding: Parent-Child Relations Across the Life Course (New York: Aldine de Gruyter, 1990), A. S. Rossi and P. H. Rossi report on the frequency and content of inter-generational relationships. They find that mothers are more likely than fathers to maintain close relationships with adult children.

17 W. Stroebe and M. S. Stroebe, "Determinants of adjustment to bereave-ment in younger widows and widowers," in M. S. Stroebe, W. Stroebe, and R. O. Hansson, eds., Handbook of Bereavement: Theory, Research, and Intervention (Cambridge: Cambridge University Press, 1993), pp. 208–226.

18 B. Wheaton's groundbreaking work on role transitions and role histories establishes a theoretical model and empirical evidence for the relief effect following dissolution of relationships with difficult role histories in "Life transitions, role histories, and mental health," American Sociological Review 55 (1990): 209–223.

19 I explain how social relationships serve to control and manage health behaviors of individuals in "Family status and health behaviors: Social control as a dimension of social integration," Journal of Health and Social Behavior 228 (1987): 306–319.

20 From Ruth Gruber, Haven: The Dramatic Story of 1,000 World War II Refugees and How They Came to America (New York: Random House, 2000), p. 30. Reprinted with the permission of Random House, Inc. Copyright © 2000 by Ruth Gruber.

21 Many sociological and psychological theories view parents as the most in-fluential players in shaping the developing child's sense of self. See reviews in N. Cantor and S. Zirkel, "Personality, cognition, and purposive behav-ior," in L. A. Pervin, ed., Handbook of Personality: Theory and Research (New York: Guilford Press, 1990), pp. 135–164, and H. Markus and S. Cross, "The interpersonal self," in ibid., pp. 576–608.

22 From Nick Hornby, High Fidelity (New York: Penguin Putnam, 1995), p. 256. Reprinted with the permission of Penguin Putnam, Inc. Copyright © 1995 by Nick Hornby.

CHAPTER 3

1 From Sylvia Plath, "Daddy," in Ariel (New York: HarperCollins,1961), p. 56. Copyright 1963 by Ted Hughes. Permission granted by HarperCollins Publishers.

2   See M. Rosenberg's *Conceiving the Self* (New York: Basic Books, 1979) for a discussion of development of the self in childhood. M. P. Atkinson discusses the continuing influence of parents on the child's sense of self in adulthood in "Conceptualizations of the parent-child relationship: Attachments, crescive bonds, and identity salience," in J. A. Mancini, ed., *Aging Parents and Adult Children* (Lexington, Mass.: D. C. Heath, 1989), pp. 81–97. R. Simon provides a basic theoretical model as well as empirical support for the importance of role meanings for mental health in "The meanings individuals attach to role identities and their implications for mental health," *Journal of Health and Social Behavior* 38 (1997): 256–274.

3   N. Cantor and S. Zirkel, "Personality, cognition, and purposive behavior," in L. A. Pervin, ed., *Handbook of Personality: Theory and Research* (New York: Guilford Press, 1990), pp. 135–164.

4   The results reported in this chapter (on group differences and on the effects of symbolic images on recovery and distress) are based on an analysis of the combined in-depth interview sample and the local survey sample. See the Appendix for additional information on samples, measurement, and statistical analysis. Some of the findings and ideas presented in this chapter, as well as additional information about the statistical analysis, were first presented in D. Umberson and T. Terling, "The symbolic meaning of relationships: Implications for psychological distress following relationship loss," *Journal of Social and Personal Relationships* 14 (1997): 723–744.

5   See a discussion of the concept of generativity in D. P. McAdams and E. de St. Aubin, *Generativity and Adult Development: How and Why We Care for the Next Generation* (Washington, D.C.: American Psychological Association, 1998).

6   From Diane Wood Middlebrook, *Anne Sexton: A Biography* (New York: Random House, 1991), p. 47. Reprinted with the permission of Houghton Mifflin Company. Copyright © 1991 by Diane Wood Middlebrook.

7   From Joyce Carol Oates, *We Were the Mulvaney's* (New York: Penguin Putnam, 1996), p. 428. Reprinted with the permission of Penguin Putnam, Inc. Copyright © 1996 by The Ontario Review, Inc.

8   C. M. Sanders, "Risk factors in bereavement outcome," in M. S. Stroebe, W. Stroebe, and O. Hansson, eds., *Handbook of Bereavement: Theory, Research, and Intervention* (Cambridge: Cambridge University Press, 1993), pp. 255–267.

CHAPTER 4

1   L. K. George provides an overview of changes in demographic trends in key life course markers over time in "Sociological perspectives on life

transitions," *Annual Review of Sociology* 19 (1993): 353–373. Also, con-cerning gender differences in life course markers, see P. Moen, "Gender, age, and the life course," in *Handbook of Aging and the Social Sciences*, 4th ed. (New York: Academic Press, 1996), pp. 171–187.

2   J. Kiecolt, "Stress and the decision to change oneself: A theoretical model," *Social Psychology Quarterly* 57 (1994): 49–63.

3   N. Cantor and S. Zirkel, "Personality, cognition, and purposive behav-ior," in L. A. Pervin, ed., *Handbook of Personality: Theory and Research* (New York: The Guilford Press, 1990), pp. 135–164.

4   R. Helson and A. Stewart, "Personality change in adulthood," in T. F. Hetherton and J. L. Weinberger, eds., *Can Personality Change?* (Washington, D. C.: American Psychological Association, 1994), p. 177.

5   H. Markus and S. Cross, "The interpersonal self," in Pervin, ed., *Handbook of Personality*, pp. 576–608.

6   T. A. Rando, *Treatment of Complicated Mourning* (Champaign, Ill.: Research Press, 1993), p. 57.

7   From Katherine Graham, *Personal History* (New York: Random House, 1997), p. 257.

8   Psychologist Camille Wortman and colleagues develop this argument in C. B. Wortman, R. C. Silver, and R. C. Kessler, "The meaning of loss and ad-justment to bereavement," in M. S. Stroebe, W. Stroebe, and O. Hansson, eds., *Handbook of Bereavement: Theory, Research, and Intervention* (Cambridge: Cambridge University Press, 1993), pp. 349–366.

CHAPTER 5

1   The questions used to measure marital quality measures are presented in the Appendix. I considered the effects of parent loss on emotional support from one's partner, negative behavior by one's partner (e.g., drinking too much, having affairs), overall marital harmony, relationship strain, and fre-quency of conflict with one's partner. I compared the marriages of bereaved individuals with those of nonbereaved individuals to determine how much change in marital quality over time is due to a parent's death. This ana-lytic strategy is critical because marital quality may change for any couple, whether or not a death has occurred. By including a nonbereaved group for comparison, I can ascertain whether change in marital quality is directly linked to a parent's death. Some of the material in this chapter, as well as statistical effects reported in this chapter, were previously published in D. Umberson, "Marriage as support or strain? Marital quality following the

death of a parent," *Journal of Marriage and the Family* 57 (1995): 709–723. Also see the Appendix for statistical information.

2   Supportive relationships are equally important to the psychological well-being of men and women, but women have more supportive relationships than men do. For a study and review of research on gender differences in relationships, see D. Umberson, M. Chen, J. S. House, K. Hopkins, and E. Slaten, "The effect of social relationships on psychological well-being: Are men and women really so different?" *American Sociological Review* 61 (1996): 837–857.

3   In *The Presentation of Self in Everyday Life* (Garden City, N.Y.: Doubleday, 1959), Erving Goffman describes the family as a "backstage" where all sorts of behaviors and feelings that are not expressed outside the home may be comfortably expressed.

4   M. K. Hinchcliffe, P. W. Vaughan, D. Hooper, and F. J. Roberts discuss how a depressed spouse adversely affects the nondepressed spouse in "The melancholy marriage: An inquiry into the interaction of depression: II. Expressiveness," *British Journal of Medical Psychology* 50 (1977): 125–142. J. D. McLeod and D. A. Eckberg show empirically that depression in a spouse undermines marital quality in "Concordance for depressive disorders and marital quality," *Journal of Marriage and the Family* 55 (1993): 733–746. Also see J. C. Coyne, R. C. Kessler, M. Tal, J. Turnbull, C. B. Wortman, and J. F. Greden, "Living with a depressed person," *Journal of Consulting and Clinical Psychology* 55 (1987): 347–352.

5   The basic premise of Bowen's approach is that any change in the family system elicits change in all parts of the system until balance can be restored. See M. Bowen, "Family reaction to death," in P. Guerin, ed., *Family Therapy* (New York: Gardner, 1976), pp. 335–348. E. R. Shapiro also applies family systems theory to understanding the consequences of a family member's death for the family in *Grief as a Family Process: A Developmental Approach to Clinical Practice* (New York: Guilford Press, 1994), pp. 335–348.

CHAPTER 6

1   E.H. Erikson, *Identity: Youth and Crisis* (New York: Norton, 1968), p. 141.

2   This definition of generativity is from D. P. McAdams, "Can personality change? Levels of stability and growth in personality across the life span," in T. F. Hetherton and J. L. Weinberger, eds., *Can Personality Change?* (Washington, D.C.: American Psychological Association, 1994), pp. 299–313. Erikson's stage theory is presented in E. H. Erikson, *Childhood and Society*, 2nd ed. (New York: Norton, 1968).

3   K. Kotre, *Outliving the Self: Generativity and the Interpretation of Lives* (Baltimore: Johns Hopkins University Press, 1984), p. 10. A theoretical framework for understanding generativity is also provided in "The anatomy of generativity," in D. P. McAdams and E. de St. Aubin, eds., *Generativity and Adult Development* (Washington, D.C.: American Psychological Association, 1998), pp. 7–43. Much of this work on generativity builds on Earnest Becker's theoretical perspective on "the denial of death." See E. Becker, *The Denial of Death* (New York: Free Press, 1973).

4   Some of the statistical effects reported in this chapter were previously published in D. Umberson, "Demographic position and stressful midlife events: Effects on the quality of parent/child relationships," in C. D. Ryff and M. M. Seltzer, eds., *The Parental Experience in Midlife* (Chicago: University of Chicago Press, 1996), pp. 493–531.

5   D. Umberson, "Family status and health behaviors: Social control as a dimension of social integration," *Journal of Health and Social Behavior* 228 (1987): 306–319.

6   F. E. Kobrin and G. E. Hendershot, "Do family ties reduce mortality? Evidence from the United States, 1966–1968," *Journal of Marriage and the Family* 39 (1977): 737–745; R. Weatherall, H. Joshi, and S. Macran, "Double burden or double blessing? Employment, motherhood, and mortality in the longitudinal study of England and Wales," *Social Science and Medicine* 38 (1994): 285–297.

CHAPTER 7

1   O. Hemstrom, "Is marriage dissolution linked to differences in mortality risks for men and women?" *Journal of Marriage and the Family* 58 (1996): 366–378. Hemstrom's calculations take into account socioeconomic status, labor force participation, and presence of children in the home. For an in-depth discussion on the effects of widowhood on health, see W. Stroebe and M. S. Stroebe, *Bereavement and Health: The Psychological and Physical Consequences of Partner Loss* (Cambridge: Cambridge University Press, 1987). Regarding widowhood and physical health consequences, see M. Murphy, K. Glaser, and E. Grundy, "Marital status and long-term illness in Great Britain," *Journal of Marriage and the Family* 59 (1997): 156–164.

2   M. Perlmutter and E. Hall, *Adult Development and Aging* (New York: John Wiley and Sons, 1992), pp. 329–334.

3   See a review of research on caregiving in C. Aneshensel, L. I. Pearlin, J. T. Mullan, S. H. Zarit, and C. J. Whitlatch, *Profiles in Caregiving: The Unexpected Career* (San Diego: Academic Press, 1995).

4   W. Stroebe and M. S. Stroebe, *Bereavement and Health* (1987); D. Umberson, C. B. Wortman, and R. C. Kessler, "Widowhood and depression: Explaining long-term gender differences in vulnerability," *Journal of Health and Social Behavior* 33 (1992): 10–24.

5   Stroebe and Stroebe, *Bereavement and Health* (1987).

CHAPTER 8

1   R. Pianta, B. Egeland, and M. F. Erickson report that parents' perceptions of a particular child as having a "difficult temperament" is associated with abuse of that child in "The antecedents of treatment: Results of the mother-child interaction research project," in D. Cicchetti and V. Carlson, eds., *Child Maltreatment* (New York: Cambridge University Press, 1989), pp. 203–253.

2   C. S. Aneshensel, L. I. Pearlin, J. T. Mullan, S. H. Zarit, and C. J. Whitlatch, *Profiles in Caregiving: The Unexpected Career* (San Diego: Academic Press, 1995), pp. 18–27.

3   Census data indicate that the need for assistance with activities of daily living increases with age: from 9.3 percent of sixty-five- to sixty-nine-year-olds to 45.4 percent of those aged eighty-five and older (reported in Aneshensel et al., *Profiles in Caregiving*, p. 6).

CHAPTER 9

1   A. S. Rossi and P. H. Rossi, *Of Human Bonding: Parent-Child Relations Across the Life Course* (New York: Aldine de Gruyter, 1990).

2   N. Chodorow, *The Reproduction of Mothering* (Berkeley: University of California Press, 1978).

3   T. A. Rando, *Treatment of Complicated Mourning* (Champaign, Ill.: Research Press, 1993), p. 57.

4   C. B. Wortman, R. C. Silver, and R. C. Kessler, "The meaning of loss and adjustment to bereavement," in M. S. Stroebe, W. Stroebe, and O. Hansson, eds., *Handbook of Bereavement: Theory, Research, and Intervention* (Cambridge: Cambridge University Press, 1993), pp. 349–366.

5   From Valerie Steiker, *The Leopard Hat* (New York: Pantheon, 2002), p. 262. Reprinted with the permission of Pantheon Books, a division of Random House, Inc. Copyright © 2002 by Valerie Steiker.

6   B. Raphael, W. Middleton, N. Martinek, and V. Misso, "Counseling and therapy of the bereaved," in Stroebe et al., eds., *Handbook of Bereavement*, pp. 427–453.

7   Human agency is a central principle of life course research. Individuals are affected by their environments, but they are viewed as having the potential and motivation to direct the course of their own lives within the constraints of any particular context. See, e.g., G. H. Elder, "Time, human agency and social change: Perspectives on the life course," *Social Psychology Quarterly* 57 (1994): 4–15; L. K. George, "Sociological perspectives on life transitions," *Annual Review of Sociology* 19 (1993): 353–373; and P. Moen, "Gender, age, and the life course," in *Handbook of Aging and the Social Sciences*, 4th ed. (New York Academic Press, 1996), pp. 171–187.

8   Also see D. R. Lehman, D. Ellard, and C. B. Wortman, "Social support for the bereaved: Recipients' and providers' perspectives on what is helpful," *Journal of Consulting and Clinical Psychology* 2 (1986): 344–367.

9   These results are based on an analysis of the 1986, 1989, and 1994 interviews with respondents in the national surveys. See the Appendix for additional information on the statistical analysis.

10 These results are based on an analysis of closed-ended questions with the in-depth interview respondents.

APPENDIX

1   J. S. House, "Americans' changing lives: Wave I," electronic data tape and producer, Ann Arbor, Mich., Survey *Research Center; Director,* Ann Arbor, Mich., Inter-University Consortium for Political and Social Research, 1986.

2   L. Radloff, "The CES-D Scale: A self-report depression scale for research in the general population," *Applied Psychological Measurement* 1 (1977): 385–401.

3   L. F. Berkman and L. Breslow, *Health and Ways of Living* (New York: Oxford University Press, 1983).

4   D. Umberson and M. Chen, "Effects of a parent's death on adult children: Relationship salience and reactions to loss," *American Sociological Review* 59 (1994): 152–168; D. Umberson, "Marriage as support or strain? Marital quality following the death of a parent," *Journal of Marriage and the Family* 57 (1995): 709–723; D. Umberson, "Demographic position and stressful midlife events: Effects on the quality of parent-child relationships," in C. D. Ryff and M. M. Seltzer, eds., *The Parental Experience in Midlife* (Chicago: University of Chicago Press, 1996), pp. 493–531.

5   E. Babbie, *The Practice of Social Research*, 5th ed. (Belmont, Calif.: Wadsworth, 1989).

6   S. Stryker, *Symbolic Interactionism: A Social Structural Version* (Menlo Park, Calif.: Benjamin Cummings, 1980).

7   C. Marshall and G. B. Rossman, *Designing Qualitative Research* (Newbury Park, Calif.: Sage, 1989).

8   D. Umberson and T. Terling, "The symbolic meaning of relationships: Implications for psychological distress following relationship loss," *Journal of Social and Personal Relationships* 14 (1997): 723–744.

INDEX

alcohol, 24, 34–41; children and, 144; early conditioning and, 34–37, 195–9; emotional expression and, 47; father's death and, 36–41, 195–6; health decline and, 25; measurement of, 225–6; reduction in, 37–41; sleep and, 24; spousal role in, 37–8; symbolism and, 71–3, 200
avoidance, 23

Becker, Ernest, 17
bereavement: advice for, 212–16; empathy and, 113–16, 126–8, 133–4, 172–3, 180–7 encouragement and, 204–11; grief and, 116–18 (see also grief); health and, 24–6, 216–17; identification and, 81–90, 93–4, 217–20; individuality and, 13–14, 204–6; length of, 230; marriage effects and, 105–30 (see also marital quality); mentors and, 62–3; negative memories and, 85–91; parental symbols and, 49–51, 77–8; recovery expectations and, 116–17; resolution and, 41–5, 216–17; role reversal and, 134–5, 167–8; siblings and, 171–93

(see also siblings); statistical rate of, 15–16; steadying influences and, 144–7; vulnerability and, 138–41; widowhood and, 151–70; see also coping strategies; emotion

Cantor, Nancy, 80
care-giving, 29, 52; impaired parents and, 189–92; role reversal and, 134–5, 167–9; siblings and, 171–93
case studies: Abigail, 213; Adam, 135; Alejandro, 58–9, 196; Amber, 74–5; Angie, 214; Bill, 29, 89–90, 109–10, 154–5; Bobby, 96, 111–12, 136, 155–6, 201, 206; Bridget, 65–6; Carol, 97; Casey, 184–6; Charles, 101–2; Christine, 96–7; Cindy, 110–11, 208; Claire, 64; Clara, 187; Connie, 178, 209; Dan, 85–6, 213; David, 76, 146–7; Desley, 93–4, 125, 215; Diana, 174–5, 177; Diane, 41–3, 69–72; Dorie, 203; Eileen, 205; Ella, 147, 159–62; George, 34–7, 197–8, 200; Ginger, 1–3, 119, 167–9, 204; Glenn, 209; Greg, 76–7, 176, 203, 205; Hannah, 57, 66–7; Helen, 22, 83–4, 135, 164–5, 181; Jackie,

case studies (*cont.*):
127–8, 178–9, 189, 210; James,
23–4; Jeannie, 28–9, 162–3; Jen,
52–3; Jenna, 148–9; Joan, 139,
186; Jody, 37–8; Joel, 205;
Jonathon, 20–1, 60–1, 168; Joyce,
176–7; Judy, 214; Karen, 88–9,
94–5; Kim, 39–40, 53, 84, 218–19;
Kit, 147–8; Lois, 32–3, 44–5,
106–8, 110, 134, 143, 157–8;
Lorrie, 72–3, 198; Lynn, 114–15,
133–4, 142, 194, 205–6, 219;
Marilyn, 159; Mark, 142–3, 200;
Marsha, 153–4; Marta, 172–3;
Mary, 67–9, 187–8; Matt, 213;
Max, 204; Michael, 114, 116–17,
144–5; Michelle, 97–8, 126–7;
Narda, 206–7; Nathan, 208; Nina,
99–101, 117–18; Patricia, 188–9;
Patty, 137–8; Paula, 122–3, 201;
Rebecca, 63–5, 112, 119–22,
136–7, 200, 207, 212–13; Rhoda,
163–4, 190; Richard, 141; Sandy,
139–40; Sharon, 126, 191; Sherry,
196; Stephanie, 43–4, 115–16,
175–6; Steven, 112–13, 173–4;
Susan, 86–7, 95–6, 145–6; Terri,
30–1, 177–8, 190, 216; Thomas,
195; Tina, 32, 140–1, 181–3,
191–2, 210, 215; Todd, 59–61;
Tom, 90–3, 200, 218; Veronica,
218; Warren, 62–3
Center for Epidemiological Studies
Depression Scale, 225, 228, 233
children, adult: as concerned parents,
138–41; care-giving and, 29, 52,
171–93; dysfunctional parent and,
41–5, 71–2, 197–8; early
conditioning and, 26, 34–37,
41–45, 49–50, 195–9; generativity
and, 131–50; health decline and,
24–6; identification and, 81–90,
93–4, 217–20; loss of youth, 61,
94–7; marital quality and, 105–30;
marriage and, 38, 57–8, 105
(*see also* marital quality); maternal
closeness and, 26–7; medical
decisions and, 101–2; need for love
and, 72–5; parenting strategies
and, 138–43; parent's opinion of
spouse and, 115–16; reciprocal
giving and, 75–7; rites of passage
and, 8–9, 194–220 (*see also* rites of
passage); role reversal and, 134–5,
167–9; self-mortality and, 49–50,
97–8; siblings and, 171–93;
symbolic loss and, 49–79; turning
points and, 79–104; widowhood of
parent and, 151–70
children, young, 227; closer
relationships with, 133–4;
generativity and, 131–50;
increased focus on, 131–2; role
reversal and, 134–5
Chodorow, Nancy, 19, 198–9
coping strategies: alcohol and, 24
(*see also* alcohol); avoidance and,
19, 23; children and, 144–7;
compartmentalization and, 19;
directing personal change and,
211–12; escaping parent, 91–3;
gender and, 20–3, 197–8; grief
expression and, 204–6; health
decline and, 24–6; identification
and, 81–90, 93–4, 217–20; letting
go of guilt, 207–8; parental
criticism and, 65–9; professional
help and, 211; psychological
distress and, 18–23; recovery and,
216–17; rejecting parent, 93–4;
relationship improvement and,
206–7; relief, 31–4, 197–8;